Frustration and Aggression

FRUSTRATION

AND

AGGRESSION

BY

JOHN DOLLARD   NEAL E. MILLER
LEONARD W. DOOB   O. H. MOWRER
ROBERT R. SEARS

IN COLLABORATION WITH

CLELLAN S. FORD   CARL IVER HOVLAND
RICHARD T. SOLLENBERGER

YALE UNIVERSITY PRESS · NEW HAVEN AND LONDON

CONTENTS

FOREWORD vii

ACKNOWLEDGMENTS ix

I. DEFINITIONS 1

II. PSYCHOLOGICAL PRINCIPLES: I 27

III. PSYCHOLOGICAL PRINCIPLES: II 39

IV. SOCIALIZATION IN AMERICA 55

V. ADOLESCENCE 91

VI. CRIMINALITY 110

VII. DEMOCRACY, FASCISM, AND COMMUNISM . . . 142

VIII. A PRIMITIVE SOCIETY: THE ASHANTI 172

REFERENCES 191

INDEX 203

FOREWORD

This book, first printed in 1939, was written for the purpose of formulating, and citing evidence to support, a basic principle of human and animal behavior of far-reaching significance. It has stimulated a great deal of research by psychologists and other social scientists. It has proved valuable as a conceptual framework for making sense out of a wide variety of behavior.

A few years ago I suggested to the authors that a revised edition be prepared primarily for bringing the theoretical chapters more in line with the results of recent research and advancements in behavior theory. Further, a new chapter on the values of frustration and aggression might have been added to avoid leaving the impression that frustration is always bad. For example, the thwarting of a goal response is precisely a prime condition that gives rise to thinking, reasoning, and striving. It was decided, however, that the theoretical formulation had already served its purpose of challenging research; and that the chapters on socialization and adolescence were sufficient to indicate the inevitable necessity of, if not the value of, frustrating goal responses formed earlier in life, in order that new and more mature ones can be learned.

The book is still timely because aggression is a timely topic. The chapters on socialization, adolescence, criminality, and on democracy, fascism, and communism are very pertinent to many of the most challenging and puzzling problems of today. Of particular significance are the treatments of Marxian doctrine and race relations.

Although psychologists may not be agreed on the causal relations between frustration and the manifold forms of aggressive behavior, yet they are agreed that when one sees

Foreword

aggression it is well worth while to look for a thwarted desire, aspiration, promise, hope, or some other motive. Notice also that the goal toward which aggressive behavior is most likely to be directed is that of inflicting punishment, embarrassment, or injury upon someone, or damaging something or someone, valued by the aggressor.

MARK A. MAY

August 1960

ACKNOWLEDGMENTS

Among the many investigators who have struggled with the problem of frustration and aggression special acknowledgment must be made to Sigmund Freud who more than any other scientist has influenced the formulation of our basic hypothesis. We are also grateful to our colleagues in the Institute of Human Relations who have assisted in developing the community of ideas out of which this volume has been crystallized; and in particular to Professor Clark L. Hull who has demonstrated in his own work that the method of inquiry which we have adopted can be used effectively in the systematic study of behavior.

For permission to quote from the published works of many writers acknowledgment is made to the following publishers: American Council on Education; D. Appleton-Century Company; The Clarendon Press; Clark University Press; Harcourt, Brace and Company; Henry Holt and Company; Houghton Mifflin Company; H. M. Stationery Office; International Publishers Co.; Charles H. Kerr and Company; J. B. Lippincott Company; Little, Brown and Company; Longmans, Green and Company; University of Chicago Press; The University of North Carolina Press; University of Pennsylvania, Department of History; Department of Commerce, Bureau of the Census, Washington; Charles Scribner's Sons; and Yale University Press.

FRUSTRATION AND AGGRESSION

CHAPTER I

DEFINITIONS

THE problem of aggression has many facets. The individual experiences difficulty in controlling his own temper and often sees others carrying on an unwitting struggle with their hostilities. He fears justified revenge or writhes at the blow or taunt that appears from an unexpected source. Children are often expert at annoying their elders by sly mischief or a sudden tantrum. Helpless minorities are persecuted. The lynching mob has a grimness and cruelty not to be expected from people who are so gentle and kind in other situations. Primitive tribesmen slay one another and even civilized people are frightened by the prospect of new and increasingly destructive wars. This book represents an attempt to bring a degree of systematic order into such apparently chaotic phenomena.

THE BASIC POSTULATE

THIS study takes as its point of departure the assumption that *aggression is always a consequence of frustration*. More specifically the proposition is that the occurrence of aggressive behavior always presupposes the existence of frustration and, contrariwise, that the existence of frustration always leads to some form of aggression. From the point of view of daily observation, it does not seem unreasonable to assume that aggressive behavior of the usually recognized varieties is always traceable to and produced by some form of frustration. But it is by no means so immediately evident that, whenever frustration occurs, aggression of some kind and in some degree will inevitably result. In many adults and even children, frustration may be followed so promptly by an appar-

ent acceptance of the situation and readjustment thereto
that one looks in vain for the relatively gross criteria ordinarily thought of as characterizing aggressive action. It must
be kept in mind, however, that one of the earliest lessons human beings learn as a result of social living is to suppress and
restrain their overtly aggressive reactions. This does not
mean, however, that such reaction tendencies are thereby an-
nihilated; rather it has been found that, although these reactions may be temporarily compressed, delayed, disguised,
displaced, or otherwise deflected from their immediate and
logical goal, they are not destroyed. With this assumption
of the inevitability of aggression following frustration, it is
possible to bring a new measure of integration into a variety
of types of facts which have hitherto been considered more or
less isolated phenomena and to consider reasonable many instances of human conduct that have commonly been regarded
and lightly dismissed as simply irrational, perverse, or abnormal.

The plausibility of the systematic position just suggested
—which will be more fully developed in subsequent pages—
is, of course, dependent to an important degree upon the formal definitions which are given to frustration, aggression,
and certain related concepts; and an attempt will be made to
provide these terms with as high a degree of exactness and
operational specificity as possible. Formal terminology in
this field, however, is still so new and unsettled that it is necessary to rely at least in a supplementary way upon the use
of denotative examples in order to convey intended meanings
in many instances. In this and subsequent chapters, therefore,
frequent recourse is had to illustrative materials, a procedure
which in no sense is intended to constitute proof of the propositions being elucidated. Evidence of a more compelling character is not entirely lacking and will be presented from time
to time; but even this latter material should be regarded also
as evidence, not as proof. The whole intent and aim of this

book may be said, in fact, to be simply the exploration, in both a logical and empirical sense, of the implications and applications of a particular hypothesis which, despite its apparent plausibility and usefulness, is to be regarded as still an *hypothesis*.

FUNDAMENTAL CONCEPTS

AT three-thirty on a hot afternoon the bell of an ice-cream vendor is heard on the street. James, aged four, runs toward his mother and announces: "Mother, the ice-cream man! I want an ice-cream cone!" Then he looks up very appealingly, puckers his lips, grasps his mother's skirt, and starts tugging her toward the front door.

At this point an observer who had been studying the behavior of this family might make a prediction. He might say: "Now James is going to try to take his mother out to the push cart. He may attempt to take her down the right or the left branch of the walk. In either case we can say that, unless something stops him, he will be holding a cone in his hand within three minutes and will have consumed it within ten. The act of consuming the cone will put an end to the sequence which I am predicting."

It is probable, however, that such an observer would find it more convenient for his purpose to deal abstractly with some of the significant aspects of the situation than with the actual events themselves. In referring to the origin of James' behavior sequence he might say, in the terminology to be used in this book, that James is *instigated* to take his mother out to buy him an ice-cream cone. An *instigator* is some antecedent condition of which the predicted response is the consequence. It may be directly observable as in the case of the vendor's bell; or it may be an internal condition that can only be inferred—in this instance from James' statement that he wants ice cream. The statement itself is not the instigator, of course, but it may be used to indicate that an instigator exists because on previous occasions the statement has been observed to be correlated with the predicted response. The bell and the vendor are likewise interpreted as instigators because of such a previously observed correlation. The concept of instigator is clearly much broader than that of stimulus; whereas the latter refers only to energy (as physically defined) exerted on a sense-organ, the former refers to any antecedent condition, either observed or inferred, from which the response can be predicted, whether this condition be a stimulus, a verbally reported image, idea, or motive, or a state of deprivation.

The directly observable instigators to James' behavior are the bell and the ice-cream vendor. But the presence of internal instigators not directly observed could be inferred from what James says and does. To the extent that specific predictions could be made from the *appealing look*, the *puckering of the lips*, the *tugging on the skirt*, and the *statement* "I want an ice-cream cone!" that efforts would be made to get the ice cream, there would be justification for inferring the existence of instigators. All that is necessary, in order to infer their presence, is for the organism to have revealed some measurable, or at least denotable, behavior which has been shown previously to be correlated with the occurrence of the predicted response. Any refinements in either observational technique or theoretical analysis that enable one to predict responses more accurately also improve the inferences concerning the presence of instigators.

Several instigators to a certain response may operate simultaneously, and their combined effect represents the total amount of instigation to the response.[1] Instigation, therefore, is a quantitative concept and so some consideration must be given to the problem of *strength of instigation*. This strength is measured by the degree to which the instigated response competes successfully with simultaneously instigated incom-

1. In fact a number of antecedent conditions must sometimes *all* be present before any instigation occurs.

patible responses, or in different technical words, by the pre-
potency of the instigated responses.

James might notice that the lawn sprinkler was spraying
water in such a way as to cut off his path to the ice-cream
vendor. He might say that he did not want to get wet or display other behavior from which it could be inferred that there
was instigation to avoid the sprinkler. Owing to the position
of the sprinkler, this instigation would be incompatible with
the instigation to get an ice-cream cone. On one occasion
James might walk in the path of the sprinkler and on another
he might not; the instigation to have an ice-cream cone would
have competed successfully with the same simultaneous instigation to an incompatible response in the first case and not
in the second. The instigation to obtain a cone, therefore,
might be said to have been stronger when James ran through
the water than when he did not. Any conditions which allow
one to predict that James will run through more or less water
to reach the cone are conditions from which an increase or
decrease in the strength of instigation may be inferred.

In many instances of everyday behavior it is impractical to
determine directly by an obstruction technique the degree to
which simultaneously instigated incompatible responses can
be overcome. In such instances it is desirable to use certain
subsidiary measures for inferring the strength of instigation
to the predicted response. The speed, duration, force, and
probability of occurrence of a given response are presumably
functions of the degree to which the response competes successfully with simultaneously instigated incompatible responses. Under properly constant conditions, these indicators
may be used in lieu of the more exact measure. If James ran
immediately and very rapidly toward the ice-cream vendor,
it would be proper to assume that the instigation to this response was fairly strong. If, on the contrary, he dawdled, it
would be reasonable to assume that the instigation to get ice
cream was relatively weak.

In the example that has been cited, it has been said that the act of consuming the cone would put an end to the predicted sequence of behavior. This means that James is known, from observation of previous ice-cream episodes, to be very much less likely to respond to the ringing of the bell with the predicted sequence of behavior for some time after he has had an ice-cream cone than he was before eating the cone. An act which terminates a predicted sequence will be called a *goal-response*. The goal-response may be defined as that reaction which reduces the strength of instigation to a degree at which it no longer has as much of a tendency to produce the predicted behavior sequence. The hungry rat eats and no longer seeks food; because the behavior sequence is terminated, the eating is considered to be the goal-response. The ticket-buyer reaches the box-office, purchases his ticket, and no longer stands in line; the purchase of the ticket is therefore said to be the goal-response.

Later on, however, James may give the same appealing look, may tug his mother's skirt again, and announce he wants another ice-cream cone; thus he will be giving further evidence from which instigation can be inferred. The termination of a behavior sequence is frequently only temporary. If there is reason to believe that the instigation exists again, James will be expected to perform the predicted sequence a second time. In fact, he will be expected to be even more apt to repeat the previous acts which had led successfully to the ice cream, since goal-responses have a *reinforcing effect* that induces the learning of the acts preceding them.

So far it has been assumed that nothing goes wrong to stop James. His mother, however, may insist that he wait until dinner time for his ice cream. His father may arrive on the scene, reprimand the mother for being so indulgent, and threaten to spank James for going to the cart. Or the ice-cream man may not have any more cones. In any of these cases the expected sequence of action will be interrupted and

James will be prevented from consuming the cone. Such an interference with the occurrence of an instigated goal-response at its proper time in the behavior sequence is called a *frustration.*

Normally a series of acts ripples through without interruption, but interference may occur through punishment incident to the goal-seeking activities or through inaccessibility of the goal itself. The interference may be slight, as when a mosquito hums near a person absorbed in thought, or great, as when an individual suffers the effects of kidney disease. It is, nevertheless, the same form of interference that induces the frustration. Such expressions as "to disappoint a person," "to let someone down," "to cause pain to someone," and "to block somebody in carrying out an act" indicate that one person is imposing a frustration on another.

Neither the nature nor the origin of the interrupted behavior sequence need be considered here. It is essential only that it can be identified as in the process of occurring and that the mode of interference be specified. The goal-response may involve gross overt activity such as the manipulation of a physical object or it may involve but little overt activity as in the case of receiving congratulations for work well done. And it is irrelevant whether thumb-sucking in an eighteen-months-old child occurs as an unlearned response, or whether the physical integrations necessary to it have been learned in other stimulus contexts. To have the object-manipulation or the receiving of congratulations or the thumb-sucking blocked, however, constitutes a frustration. The instigations remain and the adequate goal-responses are interdicted. In order to say that a frustration exists, then, one must be able to specify two things: (1) that the organism could have been expected to perform certain acts, and (2) that these acts have been prevented from occurring.

It must be noted here that either the goal-response of eating the ice cream or a degree of prevention caused by an interfering agent can terminate James' activity; it may be difficult to tell whether the behavior sequence has stopped because of the first or the second circumstance. This is especially true when the interfering agent is an emotional conflict within the organism itself. From an operational standpoint, however, an infallible criterion exists. A goal-response reinforces the behavior sequence leading up to it, while interference does not. If it were not known from previous experience that eating ice cream was the goal-response to James' behavior sequence, it might be difficult to tell, if interference be assumed, whether the last act carried out (e.g., giving an appealing look) before the sequence was terminated was a goal-response or not; but by determining whether this act produced a stronger tendency for James to carry out the sequence a second time a decision could be reached.

Still another concept can be gleaned from this overworked example. In the past James might always have consumed vanilla cones. Interference with this response by the fact that the vendor had no vanilla ice cream would be a frustration. A chocolate cone, however, might be found to be a more or less acceptable substitute for vanilla. A response which substitutes for the goal-response, in that it also tends to terminate and reinforce the same preceding action, is called a substitute response.

A *substitute response* is any action which reduces to some degree the strength of the instigation, the goal-response to which was prevented from occurring. It has, therefore, one property of the goal-response itself: it too can reduce the strength of instigation. This reduction may occur as a result of a quantitatively reduced goal-response, as when a child is given an opportunity to enjoy some praise for turning a somersault instead of much praise for a handspring. Or the reduction of instigation may result from the occurrence of a goal-response to some more or less discrete element of the total instigation, as when a person lights a cigarette or drinks a glass of water while awaiting a delayed luncheon.

As may be supposed, substitute responses occur with great frequency in the face of frustrations of all kinds. Eating raisin pie when there is no mince, reading romantic stories when real romance is unavailable, producing amateur theatricals when having a professional career has been prevented are characteristic substitutions. Some responses of this kind are even so apparent that they approach caricatures and are recognized by all adults in our culture—the childless woman who pampers her lap dog, the jilted lover who marries his ex-fiancée's sister, the smoker who, renouncing his practice, chews gum. These examples may give denotative definition to the concept of substitute response.[2]

Substitute responses, moreover, can be either less or more effective as terminating and reinforcing agents than the original response. To the extent that they are equally or more effective, they put an end to the frustrations preceding them and to the aggression produced by these frustrations.

At times James may kick or scream or say he hates his mother. Any such sequence of behavior, the goal-response to which is the injury of the person toward whom it is directed, is called *aggression*. According to the hypothesis, this is the primary and characteristic reaction to frustration, and will occur when something happens to interfere with James' efforts to get the ice-cream cone.

Many of the common forms of aggression can be instantly

2. *Aggressive action* may be distinguished from *substitute response* operationally. Since a substitute response reduces the instigation to the original (frustrated) goal-response, removal of the interference which caused the frustration will be followed by a reduced goal-response. Aggressive action, on the other hand, reduces only the secondary instigation to aggression set up by the frustration and does not have any effect on the strength of the original instigation. Removal of the interference following an aggressive action, therefore, will be followed by the occurrence of the original (frustrated) goal-response at its normal strength and rate.

recognized by almost any observer who belongs to Western society. Acts of physical violence are perhaps the most obvious. Phantasies of "getting even" with galling superiors or rivals, calculated forays against frustrating persons (whether the weapon is a business deal, a gun, a malicious rumor, or a verbal castigation is of little moment), and generalized destructive or remonstrative outbursts like lynchings, strikes, and certain reformist campaigns are clearly forms of aggression as well. It hardly needs special emphasis that tremendously complex learned skills, such as the use of the boomerang and machine gun, may occur in these aggressive behavior sequences.

Aggression is not always manifested in overt movements but may exist as the content of a phantasy or dream or even a well thought-out plan of revenge. It may be directed at the object which is perceived as causing the frustration or it may be displaced to some altogether innocent source or even toward the self, as in masochism, martyrdom, and suicide. The target of aggression quite as readily may be inanimate as animate, provided that the acts would be expected to produce injury were the object animate. In fact, the aggression may be undirected toward any object—a man swears after striking his thumb with a hammer—when the action would cause pain if it were directed toward a person. Such nouns as anger, resentment, hatred, hostility, animus, exasperation, irritation, and annoyance carry something of the meaning of the concept. Verbs such as destroy, damage, torment, retaliate, hurt, blow up, humiliate, insult, threaten, and intimidate refer to actions of an aggressive nature.[3]

Although the frustration-aggression hypothesis assumes a universal causal relation between frustration and aggression,

3. Aggressive behavior, like all other forms of behavior, is frequently forced into culturally defined patterns. Some of these are prohibited, some are permitted, and some are actually rewarded by social approval. A number of these patterns will be considered in more detail in Chapters IV and VIII.

it is important to note that the two concepts have been defined *independently* as well as *dependently*. The dependent
definition of aggression is *that response which follows frustration, reduces only the secondary, frustration-produced instigation, and leaves the strength of the original instigation
unaffected.* Frustration is independently defined as *that condition which exists when a goal-response suffers interference.*
Aggression is independently defined as *an act whose goal-
response is injury to an organism* (or *organism-surrogate*).[4]

*EXAMPLES OF THE
FRUSTRATION-AGGRESSION SEQUENCE*

It is not necessary for the purpose of this discussion to take
the position that frustration originally (in a genetic sense)
produces aggressive behavior. Frustration is possible as soon
as unlearned or learned reaction sequences are in operation
in the child. It would seem, therefore, that frustration can
conceivably occur during the birth process itself and at any
time thereafter. This need not be the case, however, with aggressive responses as here defined. The first reactions to frustration may indeed be of a random character and may lack
that destructiveness which is here posited for aggression. It
may also be that out of a battery of random responses to
frustration certain ones are learned as effective in reducing
the strength of the frustration-induced instigation (though
not the strength of the original instigation) and that these
later appear as aggression. Whether the relationship be
learned or innate, when the curtain rises on the theoretical
scene which is surveyed in this volume, frustration and aggression are already joined as response sequences.

4. One person may injure another by sheer accident. Such acts are not
aggression, because they are not goal-responses. In statistical investigations
accidents may be ignored since they are merely chance or attenuating factors. In the individual case it is necessary, in order to be certain of the aggressive nature of a given act, to demonstrate that it was a goal-response to
instigation to injure.

Since frustrations and aggressions are familiar elements in the immediate experience of most persons in Western society, the task of denoting the phenomena to which these terms refer is relatively easy. The following examples of frustration-aggression sequences are presented with a view to giving somewhat fuller connotation to the definitions which have been presented in the foregoing pages. They are presented, the reader is reminded again, for purposes of illustration, not proof.

1. A college student was driving to a distant city to attend a football game. It was the Big Game of the season and represented an important event in the season's social festivities. He was accompanied by a girl whose good opinion he valued highly and whom he wished to impress with his extensive plans for a weekend of parties and amusement. They became very gay and hilarious during the course of the drive and he was silently congratulating himself on the successful arrangements he had made. Suddenly a siren sounded behind him and, when he stopped, the traffic officer reprimanded him severely and in a very insulting manner for "driving like a high-school kid." The sound of the siren and the officer's intrusion immediately destroyed both his rapport with the girl and the happy anticipations he had had. As soon as he was permitted to drive ahead, he began berating the manners of the officer and telling the girl that the police in that state were notorious for their bullying methods. During the remainder of the drive he seemed to have difficulty with his car; he grated the gears frequently in shifting, refused to let other cars pass him, and made insulting comments about every policeman who came in sight (though, of course, slowing down whenever they appeared). The change in behavior here is not very baffling. The student was frustrated by being humiliated before his girl; his expectations of favorable response from her diminished. His behavior became aggressive because of his hostility toward the policeman which he could

not express directly and which kept bubbling up after the arrest.

2. Although frustration as such can occur only to an individual organism, any given frustrating condition may occur to several individuals simultaneously. In such a case, a "group" is viewed distributively rather than as a collective thing. If all or most of the individuals in a group are hungry, the "group" may be said, after this distributive fashion, to be hungry. A group of laborers, for example, had gathered around a boarding-house table at six o'clock for dinner, as was their practice at the end of the day. On ordinary days they ate without much conversation but with a fair approximation of dignity and good manners. On the day in question, the group sat down at the usual hour but no waiters appeared. There were soon murmurs of protest to the general effect that, if the landlady were to stay home, dinner could be served on time; and threats were made that they might stop boarding at that house. Gradually the self-restraints usually governing behavior at the table disappeared and there was a rhythmic stamping of feet. Someone shouted, "We want food"—the rest took up the cry and produced a tremendous uproar. Hard rolls were seized from the table and thrown at the kitchen door, presumably in the direction of the landlady. Soon the object of their aggression appeared and explained the reason for the delay. Dinner was eventually served and the unusual behavior gradually died down, but with many threats and mutterings. Frustration was induced by the inability to continue those responses habitually connected with sitting down at a table and aggressive acts assumed the form of the breaches of etiquette, vociferous demands, shouted threats, and bread-throwing.

3. A youngster, aged three, showed a markedly greater tendency to naughty behavior on Monday than on any other day of the week. This child was accustomed to see her parents daily and to receive much of their personal attention, to talk

with them, to ask innumerable questions, to be taken into arms, to be cuddled and swung by her father, to be instructed and noticed. Since her parents played the actual rôle of caretakers in her life, this smooth routine was inevitably disrupted when she was turned over to the maid. On Mondays she would say that she did not like her parents, quarrel with her little sister, wet her bed, and would cry protestingly if her parents attempted to leave her at all. The question of why Monday elicited this behavior most extensively seemed answered when the parents noticed that they were much more often away from the house on Saturday and Sunday than on any other days of the week. Their absence undoubtedly was experienced by the child as a deprivation, and her bad behavior on Monday appeared to be a reaction to the Sunday frustrations. After the parents became aware of this state of affairs, however, it was noticed that the child was naughty on some Mondays when the parents had not gone away the preceding day. By closer examination it was discovered that guests came on those weekends; even though the parents were not absent, these occasions fell into the same class in the experience of the child as those on which the parents went away. Actually, after a phase of preliminary recognition and admiration, she was thrust more into the hands of the maid, pushed out of social sight, and received very much less of her parents' attention. It then appeared that the child was experiencing a frustration on both occasions, alike when the parents completely withdrew their presence by going away and when they merely withdrew it by being preoccupied with guests. The little girl gave proof of this hypothesis by telling her parents that she did not like the guests, by saying this to the guests themselves occasionally, by suggesting naïvely that they go home, and by refusing to greet them or shake hands or kiss them when they left. So far as it was within her power, she gave them unfavorable notice. Her aggression, then, followed upon the failure of her parents to coöperate in the many responses which she made toward them when life was serene and they were present without competing interests.

4. Deviant as well as normal persons occasionally make the principles in this discussion quite visible. A man was admitted to a mental hospital because of his overpowering fear that he would kill his wife and children. He had first been informed of the existence of such tendencies in himself by dreams; later, what had at first shocked him in dreams became a matter of conscious wishes against which he had to defend himself. He finally fled into the mental hospital rather than be subjected to this temptation to injure those so near to him. In such a case the principles here advanced would require an examination of the man's life to ascertain what, if any, privations he experienced through the existence of his family. It did not require much interrogation to ascertain the truth. The problem centered around having, or not having, children. The skill-level of this individual was so low that he had no chance to increase his income, if, indeed, he were able to maintain it indefinitely at the same level. Additional children meant that the available income would have to be further subdivided, that education of the existing children would be definitely limited, that the food and shelter standards for all members of the family would be lowered, and that the risks which all were running of being truly poverty-stricken would be increased. But this man was not able, for religious reasons, to utilize contraceptive measures. His wife, therefore, was a constant sex temptation to him; he was faced with the necessity of inhibiting his repeatedly instigated sex response. As a result of his own frustrations, he came to hate those who seemed to be pressing this conflict on him, namely his wife and children, and his eventual solution was flight from the whole dilemma to a mental hospital.[5]

5. The genetic complexities of this case have been omitted for reasons of space. It was not possible to determine just why this man became completely disorganized by a conflict which others solve through deceit or simple renunciation. Clear enough, however, were his intense frustration and the fierce aggressive tendencies which followed upon it.

5. A young man who was very fond of music was attending a concert by a famous violinist. The program was a brilliant one and the young man settled down to what he anticipated would be a thoroughly enjoyable evening. In spite of his interest in the music, however, he soon became aware of the squirming and wriggling of a man sitting in front of him. For a few minutes the young man tried to ignore this distraction. When the wriggling and the consequent creaking of the seat continued unabated, however, he became very angry and finally spoke sharply to the disturber, suggesting sarcastically that the rest of the audience would appreciate his using the lobby in which to do his scratching if he had to scratch and wiggle. The young man's on-going listening responses had been blocked and he reacted with an overt aggressive kind of behavior. The phrase "on-going listening responses" expresses the conception that the organism does not merely experience a "feeling of esthetic appreciation" but is actually *behaving*. The behavior is comprised of goal responses eventuating from instigation to listen to good music.

6. A young man and his wife moved to a small town and began the process of finding a position in the social hierarchy of the city. It was important for their self-esteem as well as for the business success of the husband that this position should be as high as possible. They therefore welcomed an invitation from the wife of one of the leading bankers of the town to attend an informal party at his house. Both of the young people made every reasonable attempt to be agreeable and, in fact, succeeded very well. This success seemed to be attested by a further invitation which was accepted and which also resulted in a pleasant evening.

The observer who reported on this incident was also a witness of the expressions of satisfaction which came from both husband and wife at their successful plunge into the social mill-pond. The banker and his wife were regarded cordially and their friendliness was warmly appreciated. The same observer had, however, the opportunity to witness a sharp change in the attitudes of this young couple toward their older friends. The younger woman became critical of the appearance and clothes of the banker's wife; she seemed to notice for the first time also that the older woman displayed an unseemly flirtatious attitude toward men more youthful than herself. In the conversation of the banker there was discovered an emptiness and pomposity which had not been sensed before. Discussions with friends suddenly revealed, strangely enough, that the banker was a mere figurehead in his own bank and that he was kept there because of his wealth rather than because of his business skill or judgment. There was a complete change of front from a cordial and admiring attitude to a markedly critical and hostile one. The visits to the big house stopped and a marked bitterness remained. No explanation was given for this change.

It was a number of months before the participant observer discovered, during an intimate conversation, the cause of the reversal of feeling. After several visits to the home of the banker, the young couple had thought they perceived a growing intimacy between the two families. They also experienced some dissatisfaction at accepting so much from their older friends while not themselves returning any of the favors received. After a suitable time they asked the banker family to come to dinner, with the wish to make at least a token payment on their social debt. Difficulties, however, developed at this point. After several weeks it seemed to be impossible to find any date which would be suitable to the banker and wife, and the only conclusion to be drawn was that they did not wish to come. This left the young couple with very distressing feelings of having been patronized and of not actually existing on the social horizon of the older couple. Their reactions of humiliation were inevitable.

An analysis of these data indicates that the frustrated responses were those connected with pleasure and satisfaction at securing recognition in the social life of the small town in which the young couple's lot was cast. The frustration ensued from the refusal of leaders in the hierarchy to confirm this status by accepting a dinner invitation. The refusal was frustrating, in that it put an effective end to all further action of self-betterment in the social sphere. It was undoubtedly at this point that the reaction of the young people toward the banker and his wife changed from an amiable and friendly one to an extremely resentful one. In this case, of course, the frustration itself was concealed because every admission of the humiliation to another person was in itself experienced as frustrating.

SCOPE AND LIMITATIONS

In defining the various basic concepts and exemplifying them with the above case material it becomes evident that not only do these concepts stretch across from one scientific discipline to another but that they also have a relationship to other concepts basic to a complete systematic theory of behavior. But while every effort will be made to push the frustration-aggression hypothesis as far as it will go with reference either to individual or to social facts that are relevant to it, present knowledge does not permit a detailed linking of these concepts to others within the science of behavior.

Certain relationships which must eventually be examined stand out clearly even at the present stage of systematization. A *detailed theory of learning*, for example, must play an important rôle in any complete science of human behavior. No attempt will be made here, however, to formulate any set of assumptions which might constitute such a theory; no systematic attack will be directed toward the problem of learning itself. It will simply be assumed that human beings are capable of learning and that the learning operates according to some such principle as the law of effect (171).[6]

6. Numbers in parentheses refer to the correspondingly numbered book or periodical in the list of references, pp. 191–201.

Various consequences of frustration other than aggression will be largely ignored. *Substitute responses* and *rational problem solving* both involve extensive theoretical formulations in their own right and to examine them in detail here would be impossible. Likewise it is well known that repeated frustration reduces the tendency for the frustrated series of responses to occur on subsequent occasions. This phenomenon, *experimental extinction*, has been studied in detail by Pavlov (125) and others; but, since no work has yet been done on the relationship between experimental extinction and aggression, little can be said concerning that relationship. The problem of *anxiety* is complicated by Cannon's demonstration (29) that the known physiological components of anger and fear are practically identical. It would be important, consequently, to know the exact psychological relationships between aggression and fear or anxiety, but aside from postulating that the fear (or anticipation) of punishment can inhibit specific acts of aggression, no systematic analysis of this relationship will be undertaken.

HISTORICAL BACKGROUND

It is not the purpose of this section to give a detailed, complete historical account of the development of the frustration-aggression hypothesis; this would require an independent volume. In its grosser aspects the frustration-aggression hypothesis plays an important part in the thinking of contemporary primitive and civilized peoples and was expressed in the writings of the people of antiquity. It is, in fact, implicit in the idiom of most languages. In defining the verb "to annoy," Webster's Dictionary gives, for example, the following lines from Prior:

> Say, what can more our tortured souls *annoy*
> Than to behold, admire, and lose our joy?

Various modern psychologists and social scientists have

made more or less systematic use of the frustration-aggression hypothesis. Without being entirely explicit in his formulation, William James, for example, seems to have sensed not only the broad outlines of this hypothesis but also many of its relatively refined implications, as is indicated by the following quotation:

> In many respects man is the most ruthlessly ferocious of beasts. As with all gregarious animals, "two souls," as Faust says, "dwell within his breast," the one of sociability and helpfulness, the other of jealousy and antagonism to his mates. . . . Constrained to be a member of a tribe, he still has a right to decide, as far as in him lies, of which other members the tribe shall consist. Killing off a few obnoxious ones may often better the chances of those that remain. And killing off a neighboring tribe from whom no good thing comes, but only competition, may materially better the lot of the whole tribe. Hence the gory cradle, the *bellum omnium contra omnes,* in which our race was reared; hence the fickleness of human ties, the ease with which the foe of yesterday becomes the ally of today, the friend of today the enemy of tomorrow. . . . (71, V. 2, pp. 409–410)

Clearly, in this context, pugnacity may be equated with aggression and three points of relevance to the present systematization are made: first, that aggression is regulated by an in-group ("the tribe"); second, that aggression is expressed against those who are competitors, i.e., actual or potential frustrators; and third, that people who usually arouse only friendly feelings can produce marked aggression under certain circumstances.

McDougall has denoted the phenomena of aggression in the "instinct of combat" and he states explicitly that this instinct is aroused by "obstruction," a word that, in a psychological context, is almost an exact synonym for frustration:

> Combative behavior is, then, the expression of an instinct which is peculiar in that it has no specific object; the key that opens its

door is not a sense-impression or a sensory pattern of any kind, but rather any obstruction to the smooth progress toward its natural goal of any other instinctive striving. (100, pp. 140–141)

And he adds a quantitative principle which is of great significance:

Wherever we look in the animal kingdom, the same rule seems to obtain: in general terms, the stronger the impulse at work in an animal, the more readily is the angry combative behavior evoked by any obstruction from other creatures, if the species is at all capable of this response. (100, p. 140)

It is in the work of Freud, however, that the most systematic and extensive use of the frustration-aggression hypothesis has been made. His earlier writings contain many examples. For instance, a woman patient, frustrated by her husband, appears with death wishes toward the child who continues to represent this man in her life (47, p. 170); an adult rival who imposes a professional frustration on a man is done away with in a dream (47, p. 171); the supplanted child hates the infant who diverts the parents' attention from itself (47, pp. 172, 173, 280); and finally, the child disciplined by the parent of the same sex develops a vehement dislike of that parent (47, pp. 173–174).

In his earlier writings Freud regarded the tendency to seek pleasure and avoid pain as the basic mechanism of all mental functioning. Frustration occurred whenever pleasure-seeking or pain-avoiding behavior was blocked; aggression was the "primordial reaction" (46) to this state of affairs and was thought of as being originally and normally directed toward those persons or objects in the external world which were perceived as the source of the frustration. Freud dealt with such aberrant phenomena as deliberate self-injury and suicide, not as abrogations of the pleasure-principle, but as instances of aggression "turned inward" under the influence of anxiety (threat of punishment) (46). In this connection he was led to postulate the very important principle of *displacement*.

In recent years, however, Freud's work with masochism has led him to adopt a somewhat different position, one which involves the assumption of a *death-instinct* (48). The primary object of this instinct is the destruction of life within the individual, and its operation is the basis of masochistic tendencies. This later view assumes that external aggression is the instinct of self-destruction turned outward and not a reaction to frustration. Since such a view involves assumptions outside the scope of the present volume no use will be made of it, and our debt to Freud is entirely for his earlier writings.

Dollard (35) has formulated the general principle of frustration and aggression from these earlier Freudian writings and has applied it to a Southern community in the United States. In terms of the theory he has analyzed, for example, the reactions of the Negro caste to the frustrations imposed by the white group. As a result of this examination of a cultural situation which ordinarily is observed only sociologically, he has been able to reveal the psychological effects of the social structure upon the organization of personality and behavior. Here the use of the frustration-aggression principle has been quite explicit; in at least two great sociological systems, those of Sumner and Keller and Karl Marx, the same principle has also been employed, except that it has appeared only implicitly.

Although Sumner and Keller do not specify aggression as one of the four socializing forces, i.e., hunger, love, vanity, and ghost-fear (164, V. 1, p. 21), the problem of the source of aggression is considered in connection with "antagonistic coöperation" within the in-group (164, p. 28). Aggression is viewed not as a consequence of frustration, explicitly, but as an accompaniment of group living. The coöperativeness of the in-group persists, because it is expedient, in spite of ever-present tendencies toward hostile responses between in-group members. It is stressed that it is the "sacrifice of present freedom to realize the hunger interests, love interests and the rest" which results in the antagonisms between individuals. If the "sacrifice of present freedom" be understood in personal terms, it means an interference with responses which the individuals in a social group are instigated to carry out, an interference which is imposed by the necessities of group living. In-group aggression is presumed to be a response to such interferences. These authors stress again (164, p. 355) the fact that "antagonism is present as a condition of the struggle for existence and the competition of life"; i.e., if the "existence" of a person is threatened (frustration), he becomes antagonistic. And again, they write (164, p. 18): "Where men are existing with slight resources on the edge of catastrophe—and, except in certain favored spots, we take this to have been the original state—they are full of hostility, suspicion, and other anti-social feelings and habits." Although the frustration-aggression hypothesis is not expressly and theoretically formulated, such statements seem to be an implicit recognition of its operation.

In Marxian doctrine, the theories of the class-struggle and of the nature of the state depend to some extent, again by implication, on the frustration-aggression principle. Surplus value, the materialistic interpretation of history, the nature of ideologies, these are subjects that can be treated adequately in a somewhat pure sociological or economic frame of reference. But when Marxists have described the dynamic human interrelationships involved in the class struggle and in the preservation and destruction of the state, they have introduced unwittingly a psychological system involving the assumption that aggression is a response to frustration.

The clearest and most concise statement of the nature of the class-struggle is to be found in *The Communist Manifesto*, the general *motifs* of which pervade most of the writings of Marx and Engels. The reasoning is as follows. The proletariat can be called oppressed, i.e., frustrated, since "These laborers, who must sell themselves piecemeal, are a commodity, like every other article of commerce, and are consequently exposed to all the vicissitudes of competition, to all the fluctuations of the market"; and, "owing to the extensive use of machinery and to division of labor," their work "has lost all individual character, and, consequently, all charm" (99, p. 21). The resulting aggression "goes through various states of development":

> With its [the proletariat's] birth begins its struggle with the bourgeoisie. At first the contest is carried on by individual laborers, then by the work people of a factory, then by the operatives of one trade, in one locality, against the individual bourgeois who directly exploits them. They direct their attacks not against the bourgeois conditions of production, but against the instruments of production themselves: they destroy wares that compete with their labor, they smash to pieces machinery, they set factories ablaze, they seek to restore by force the vanished status of the workman of the Middle Ages. (99, p. 23)

This blind aggression is fruitless, since the frustration or exploitation continues to increase: "The growing competition among the bourgeois, and the resulting commercial crises, make the wages of the workers ever more fluctuating." In short, "The unceasing improvement of machinery, ever more rapidly developing, makes their livelihood more and more precarious; the collisions between individual workmen and individual bourgeois take more and more the character of collisions between two classes." As a result of these increased frustrations, the aggression assumes the following form:

> The workers begin to form combinations (trades' unions) against the bourgeois; they club together in order to keep up the rate of wages; they found permanent associations in order to make provision

beforehand for these occasional revolts. Here and there the contest breaks out into riots. (99, p. 24)

This aggression, however, is not yet completely directed against the frustrating agents, the bourgeoisie, for the "organization of the proletarians into a class, and consequently into a political party, is continually being upset again by the competition between the workers themselves." Finally, "when the class-struggle nears the decisive hour," the proletariat has organized its aggression and is "a really revolutionary class."

An extremely important instrument of the ruling class which prevents the frustrated from expressing their aggression against their frustrators is the state. It was Lenin, the practical strategist as well as Marxian theorist, who developed, as he himself has said, the implications of Marx and Engels in respect to the functioning of that state. In his *The State and Revolution*, he states plainly:

The State is the product and the manifestation of the *irreconcilability* of class antagonisms. The State arises when, where, and to the extent that the class antagonisms *cannot* be objectively reconciled. And, conversely, the existence of the State proves that the class antagonisms *are* irreconcilable. (87, p. 154; italics his)

The capitalistic state, then, with its "special bodies of armed men," enables "imperialism" and "banks" to create "to an unusually fine art both these methods of defending and asserting the omnipotence of wealth in democratic republics of all descriptions"; or, in Engels' words (which Lenin quotes with approval), the state is a "special repressive force."

It is evident that Marxian theory assumes the existence of profound frustrations in each member of the proletariat. These derive from many circumstances, among which are: the destruction of his pride by being forced to work at a machine and by being treated as another commodity; exploitation by his employers; the crises of the economic system; and the repressive measures of the state. These frustrations lead inevitably to aggression and eventually, according to the Marxian prediction, to the triumph of the oppressed class.

ALTHOUGH the various writings here discussed contain the essence of the frustration-aggression hypothesis, only Freud has presented it formally. The present work strives to continue Dollard's elaboration of this hypothesis, to carry it further, and still to remain within the frame of reference of objective, behavioral science. It differs from past attempts at systematization of behavior in that it cuts *across* fields and does not concentrate upon linking together the levels *within* any one field. In no sense can it claim to be a complete systematization of human behavior, either of the individual or the group. But it does endeavor to place within a common discourse such diverse phenomena as strikes and suicides, race prejudice and reformism, sibling jealousy and lynching, satirical humor and criminality, street fights and the reading of detective stories, wife-beating and war.

CHAPTER II

PSYCHOLOGICAL PRINCIPLES: I

THE basic hypothesis which has been presented is that aggression is always a consequence of frustration. It is clear from common observation and from a consideration of the examples of this relationship given in Chapter I, however, that aggressive behavior may take many forms. Sometimes aggression is directed at the frustrating agent; at other times it seems to be aimed at innocent bystanders. Some forms of aggression are vigorous and undisguised; others are weak or subtle and roundabout. While the simple statement that frustration produces aggression, therefore, may add something of value to the problem of predicting human behavior, other psychological factors besides frustration itself must be taken into consideration if a more adequate understanding of the specific forms that aggression takes is to be gained. In this and the succeeding chapter a more systematic analysis of four groups of factors will be made:

1. Those governing the strength of instigation to aggression; i.e., the amount of frustration.

2. Those related to the inhibition of aggressive acts; i.e., the effects of punishment.

3. Those determining the object toward which aggression is directed and the form this aggression takes; i.e., the displacement of aggression.

4. Those related to the reduction of instigation to aggression; i.e., the catharsis of aggression.

The various principles presented in these chapters are tentative and cannot pretend to deal with all the factors related to aggression. They represent an attempt to pose a problem as clearly and as systematically as possible, rather than an effort to give a final answer to the problem. They will be illustrated with a variety of clinical, sociological, and experimental data but in no sense can these data be considered as attempts to prove the propositions. Such data are included merely to make the points more intelligible and to suggest the kind of empirical evidence which is eventually necessary in order to analyze the propositions critically and to develop more adequate ones.

STRENGTH OF INSTIGATION TO AGGRESSION

THE first step in elaborating the basic hypothesis is to restate it in the following quantitative form: the strength of instigation to aggression varies directly with the amount of frustration. The next step is to consider the factors which are responsible for the amount of frustration and therefore also responsible for the strength of instigation to aggression. It is assumed that there are three such factors: *the strength of instigation to aggression should vary directly with (1) the strength of instigation to the frustrated response, (2) the degree of interference with the frustrated response, and (3) the number of frustrated response-sequences.* Each of these factors will now be discussed and illustrated.

1. *Strength of instigation to the frustrated response.* According to this principle, withdrawal of food from a hungry dog should produce more growling and baring of teeth than similar withdrawal from a satiated dog. Loss of a crucial page from a detective story should exasperate a twelve-year-old boy more than loss of an equally crucial page from his history lesson.

An appeal to common experience gives this proposition an appearance of obvious validity which relevant experimental data are not yet completely adequate to check. Those that are cited here are regarded primarily as further illustrations and not as final proofs. An experiment by Sears and Sears (144) was designed to utilize variations in the strength of a five-months-old baby's hunger instigation as the independent variable. During a three-week period, at two of the four daily feedings, the child's feeding was systematically interrupted by withdrawal of the bottle from the mouth after varying amounts of milk had been taken. With this method, frustration of sucking and eating occurred when the instigation to those acts was of several different strengths. The strength of the aggressive reaction was measured in terms of the immediacy of crying following the withdrawal. When withdrawal occurred after only .5 oz. had been taken, crying began, on the average, after 5.0 seconds; after 2.5 oz. had been taken, the latency was 9.9 seconds; and after 4.5 oz. had been taken, it was 11.6 seconds. These figures indicate that as the child became more nearly satiated, i.e., as the strength of instigation decreased, frustration induced a less and less immediate aggressive response.

Two questionnaire studies by Doob and Sears (37) and Miller (106) have yielded additional relevant data. In the first, college students were given descriptions of various frustrating situations they had encountered in real life. Below each situation was listed a series of aggressive actions and substitute responses which might have occurred in the situation. The subjects were instructed to indicate which responses they had actually made and to rate on a four-point scale the strength of the instigator whose goal-responses had suffered interference. The proportion of responses which were aggressive was reliably greater as the strength of the instigation was rated higher.[1]

The proverbial violence of lovers' quarrels is probably a consequence of this same principle. Since two lovers presumably have greater instigation to affectional behavior involving each other than two non-lovers have, interference with this behavior by one of the former produces a more serious frustration than would be the case with the latter. The con-

---

1. For a more extensive description of this study, see below, p. 35.

sequences of a somewhat similar difference in strength of instigation were illustrated in the study by Miller. He employed an annoyance test which permitted subjects to indicate the degree of annoyance caused by (*a*) being snubbed by various persons whom the subject liked to different degrees, and (*b*) being "off form" in sports for which the subject had different degrees of instigation to be successful. Ratings from a large group of college students indicated that in these situations the principle that the stronger the instigation the stronger the annoyance (aggression) held true. Being snubbed by an acquaintance was rated as more annoying than being snubbed by a stranger. Being snubbed by a close friend was, in turn, worse than being snubbed by an acquaintance. Similar results were obtained from the items pertaining to sport; the stronger the liking for a sport, the greater the annoyance exhibited at being "off form" in it. All these differences had critical ratios greater than 3.00.

2. *Degree of interference with the frustrated response.* According to this principle, a slight distraction producing a little interference with a golfer's drive at a crucial moment should be less likely to cause him to swear than a stronger distraction producing a much greater interference. Delays are also thought of as interferences. An employee, therefore, should be more likely to be severely reprimanded for keeping his busy employer waiting idly for thirty minutes than for being but three minutes tardy.

Empirical data illustrative of this second factor may be obtained from various kinds of social statistics. While these statistics undoubtedly involve a greater number of uncontrolled variables than would the results of an appropriate laboratory experiment, the facts which they represent are of such social significance that even a tentative attempt to elucidate them is of some interest.

Two correlations can be cited to demonstrate that aggression increases with an increase in interference with the goal-response. Indices of economic conditions were assumed by Hovland and Sears (69) to reflect the ease, or difficulty, with which customary economic activities of the members of a group can be carried out. Low indices, or bad economic conditions, should represent a greater interference with customary goal-responses than do high indices or good business conditions. The annual numbers of lynchings and property crimes with violence were taken as measures of aggression. As one index of the severity of interference with economic actions, the annual per acre value of cotton was computed for fourteen Southern states for the years 1882 to 1930. The correlation between this index and the number of lynchings in these same fourteen states was —.67; i.e., the number of lynchings (aggression) increased when the amount of interference increased. Similarly, Thomas (170) has found that property crimes with use of violence are correlated —.44 with economic indices.

Miller's study of annoyances (106) has also furnished results bearing on the same problem. The subjects reported that they felt much more irritated at being completely "off form" in their favorite sport than at being only slightly "off form." The critical ratio of this difference was 5.5.

3. Number of frustrated response-sequences. In addition to the variations in strength of any frustration, the amount or strength of aggressive response will depend in part on the amount of residual instigation from previous or simultaneous frustrations, which instigation summates to activate the response under observation. Minor frustrations add together to produce an aggressive response of greater strength than would normally be expected from the frustrating situation that appears to be the immediate antecedent of the aggression. The temporal factor is of great importance in this connection, but there are no data available at present to indicate precisely how long after the removal of the primary frustration the secondary instigation to aggression will persist. Further reference to this problem of "readiness to be aggressive" will be made in Chapter IV.

Morgan (113, pp. 245–246) has suggested an everyday kind of situation to indicate the potentialities (for aggression) of summation of previous frustrations:

Suppose we get up in the morning with the decision that, no matter what happens during this day, we will be sweet-tempered. In spite of our determination things may go wrong. We may stub our toe, lose our collar button, cut ourselves while shaving, be unable to find the styptic to stop the bleeding, get to breakfast late and discover that the toast is burned and the coffee cold, but through all this we keep cool and even-tempered. Then some trivial thing occurs and we unexpectedly have a violent outburst. Those around us cannot understand why we are so irritable. If they knew all the facts, the repressed anger impulses that have at last gained an outlet, they would not be so surprised.

Studies of sleep-deprivation (75; 143) indicate the ease with which minor frustrations can bring about explosions of wrath when there is a background of serious frustration. In one investigation (143) a man who had previously been a willing subject for several arduous experiments complained vigorously at having to give free associations to fifty stimulus words. Another gave zero ratings to a series of jokes and added the comment that there was a limit to what could be called funny; he rated as mildly funny similar series of dull jokes both the day before and the day after the experiment.

INHIBITION OF ACTS OF AGGRESSION

It is evident, of course, that all frustrating situations do not produce overt aggression. Few arrested motorists jeer at the policeman; guests at formal dinners do not complain when the meat is tough; German Jews do not strike Nazi storm-troopers. To assume, however, that in such cases there is no aggression would be clearly false. Careful questioning may elicit the statement that the frustrated person "feels angry" or is "annoyed" or is "simply furious inside." These verbal expressions refer to implicit or partially inhibited aggressive actions which may be called *non-overt* as opposed to the *overt* aggression of fighting, striking, swearing, and other easily observed actions. It is not supposed that these terms refer to discrete classes of aggressive behavior but simply to the extremes of a descriptive continuum.

The basic variable that determines the degree to which any specific act of aggression will be inhibited appears to be anticipation of punishment. Provisionally it may be stated that *the strength of inhibition of any act of aggression varies positively with the amount of punishment anticipated to be a consequence of that act.* A boy who has been severely spanked for hitting his little brother should be somewhat less apt to hit him again under similar circumstances.

In essence this principle derives from the law of effect; those actions cease to occur which, in the past, have been followed by punishment.[2] It may be supposed that each frustration acts as an instigator to a great variety of aggressive responses. Some of these are overt in the sense that other persons can perceive them and some are so minimal (non-overt) that only the subject himself is aware of them. If past experience has taught him that certain of these aggressions are followed by punishment, those forms will tend to be eliminated and there will remain a residue of the forms that have not been punished. The overt vs. non-overt dimension achieves its importance primarily from the fact that in our own society, as well as in many others, it is the overt aggressions which are so frequently punished.[3] It must be recognized, however, that the general principle that punishment may eliminate any specific act of aggression can apply equally

2. This "ceasing to occur" relates only to the specific form of the action and not to the occurrence of aggression itself as a response to frustration.
3. *Cf.* Chapter IV.

well, whether that act be overt, non-overt, or in some other descriptive dimension.

Some consideration must be given to a definition of punishment as it is used in this connection. There can be little question that such responses on the part of the social environment as physical injury, insults, ostracism, and deprivation of goods or freedom constitute punishment, but the term as it refers to these experiences has a connotation of "intention" on the part of the punishing persons. No such implication is essential nor is it desirable. Punishment, in essence, is equivalent to the occurrence of pain, but refers to the objective conditions of the infliction of pain rather than to facts of immediate experience.

In this sense two occurrences not ordinarily considered under the rubric of punishment may be added to the forms mentioned above. (1) *Injury to a loved object is punishment.* Since human love seems, almost universally, to involve an identification of the lover with the loved object, any punishment which the latter suffers is essentially a punishment of the lover himself. Aggression clearly has an injurious effect when it is expressed overtly and hence any aggression expressed toward the loved object serves to injure the person who has identified himself with the loved object. (2) *Anticipation of failure is equivalent to anticipation of punishment.*[4] The failure may be anticipated either because of a lack of a suitable object or because there are insuperable difficulties involved in carrying out the act.[5]

---

4. This seems to be analogous to the experimental extinction of a conditioned response and may actually follow somewhat different laws from those followed in the elimination of a response through punishment.

5. The mechanism by which anticipation of punishment operates to eliminate an action is not of paramount importance in the present context. To use the term "anticipation" in connection with strictly behavioral concepts such as goal-response, frustration, and aggression does no violence to the unity of the level of discourse provided the term "anticipation" is also defined behaviorally. Hull (70) has presented the concept of *anticipatory goal-response* to account for foresightful and purposive behavior, and Sears (142)

Evidence for the validity of the statement that anticipation of punishment inhibits overt aggression has been obtained by Doob and Sears (37). The questionnaire, mentioned above, described sixteen frustrating situations and was presented to 185 college students. Below the description of each situation were given several alternative reactions to it. The subjects were instructed to record four items of information with regard to each of the situations which they had *actually experienced* within the preceding few months: (1) how strongly they had wanted to do the thing which the frustrating situation prevented their doing (four-point rating scale), (2) which reaction to the frustration they had actually made, (3) which reaction would have been most satisfying at the time and how satisfying it would have been (four-point scale), and (4) from which reaction they would have anticipated the most punishment and how much it would have been (four-point scale). The list of possible reactions to each of the situations contained examples of overt and non-overt aggression and substitute responses.

In more than a third of the instances an overt reaction was marked as the most satisfying in anticipation but also likely to lead to the most punishment. These particular cases were divided into three groups: (1) those in which satisfaction was given a higher rating than anticipated punishment, (2) those in which the two ratings were equal, and (3) those in which the anticipation of punishment was greater than the satisfaction to be obtained. The proportion of overt responses which actually occurred decreased from Group 1 to Group 3: the obtained values were, respectively, 60.7 per cent, 50.5 per cent, 33.3 per cent. This finding supports the hypothesis that anticipation of punishment reduces overt aggression.

has shown that its use in the form of *anticipated punishment* makes it possible to cast the theory of repression into behavioral terminology. Miller (107) has demonstrated its operation in such a way as to leave little doubt that many problems involving the effect of future events on present behavior can be handled properly with the use of this concept.

CONFLICT BETWEEN INSTIGATION AND
INHIBITION

UNDERLYING the statement that anticipation of punishment decreases the degree to which any aggressive act is expressed is the assumption that the strength of instigation to the aggression is held constant. If the strength of this instigation is increased, however, it may become strong enough to overcome the anticipation of punishment. In other words, a sufficiently "infuriated" (frustrated) person may "throw caution to the winds" and attack the frustrating agent. The overcoming of the anticipation of punishment depends on the assumption that *the strengths of antagonistic or incompatible responses summate negatively in some algebraic manner*. Although this assumption may have to be qualified, Hovland and Sears (68) and Bugelski and Miller (28) have demonstrated its usefulness in the theoretical explanation of conflicts. The conflict in the present instance is between the two incompatible action-sequences of expressing a specific act of aggression and of avoiding the punishment anticipated for such expression.

Tentative evidence for assuming some form of algebraic summation of the two antagonistic factors called instigation and inhibition may be obtained from the same questionnaire study of Doob and Sears (37). Not only did the proportion of aggressive responses increase with increase in the strength of the instigation, as rated by the subjects; but also, in line with the fact that more punishment was anticipated for overt than for non-overt aggression, the proportion of aggressive acts which were overt rather than non-overt increased in the same way. Of the aggressive responses to those situations in which the drive was rated as "very weak," only 39.0 per cent were overt aggression; the next strongest rating produced 44.7 per cent overt; the next strongest, 47.6 per cent; and the strongest, 61.6 per cent. The progressive increase in the amount of overt aggression as the instigation to aggression becomes stronger is evidence that the successively stronger instigations are able to override progressively more of the inhibitions against acts of overt aggression.

The theory of trait structure, as described by Allport (7), lends justification for suggesting that *generalized habits* of responding to frustrating situations with overt or non-overt aggression may be another factor which determines the specific reactions on any given occasion. Allport has shown, with reference to other descriptive dimensions of personality, that widely differing social situations serve as equivalent instigators for behavior that can be conceptualized under a single rubric. The so-called *individual trait* represents this kind of determining tendency. On theoretical grounds, at least, there seems to be no reason why, for a given individual, frustrating situations could not serve as equivalent instigators for any degree of overt aggression. In such case it would be legitimate to speak of a *trait of overtness or non-overtness*. Preliminary indications tending to support such an hypothesis are evident in the demonstration by Miller and Goodyear (111) that overt fighting behavior in rats can be established in a specific situation by trial-and-error learning; but for this degree of overtness to be called a trait it would have to be found and tested in other situations as well.

SUMMARY

1. The strength of instigation to aggression varies directly with the amount of frustration. Variation in the amount of frustration is a function of three factors: (1) strength of instigation to the frustrated response; (2) degree of interference with the frustrated response; and (3) the number of response sequences frustrated.

2. The inhibition of any act of aggression varies directly with the strength of the punishment anticipated for the expression of that act. Punishment includes injury to loved ob-

jects and failure to carry out an instigated act as well as the usual situations which produce pain.

3. In general it may be said that, with the strength of frustration held constant, the greater the anticipation of punishment for a given act of aggression, the less apt that act is to occur; and secondly, with anticipation of punishment held constant, the greater the strength of the frustration, the more apt aggression is to occur.

CHAPTER III

PSYCHOLOGICAL PRINCIPLES: II

DIRECT AND INDIRECT AGGRESSION

IN the preceding chapter the basic hypothesis has been elaborated by considering certain factors which are presumed to influence the strength of instigation to aggression and the degree of inhibition of aggression. Additional factors that must be analyzed are those presumed to influence the direction of aggression.

In order to begin the task of describing the direction which aggression will be expected to take, it is necessary to make a further assumption: *the strongest instigation, aroused by a frustration, is to acts of aggression directed against the agent perceived to be the source of the frustration and progressively weaker instigations are aroused to progressively less direct acts of aggression.*[1] A man who has just had his vacation plans disrupted by his employer will be expected, on the basis of this assumption, to be most angry at his employer but also somewhat more irritable toward the world in general.

The principle that the strongest instigation is to aggression against the agent perceived to be the source of the frustration finds a social application in war propaganda. Lasswell (83, p. 47) has shown that one of the techniques for making people aggressive toward the enemy during the

---

1. In the absence of an acceptable stimulus-response theory of perception, this assumption must be phrased in a somewhat unsatisfactory manner. It would seem that learning which response is the most effective in removing the frustration must be an important factor in building up the type of perception upon which the definition of direct aggression is based. It would also seem that the generalization posited in this assumption is analogous to the generalization of a conditioned response: the more direct acts of aggression will be those which are more similar, or more closely bound by associational ties, to the act of most direct aggression.

World War was to make them believe that this enemy was the actual or potential source of important frustrations. Further evidence, indirectly supporting this principle, is suggested by the fact that the subjects in the study by Doob and Sears (37) definitely reported acts of direct aggression to be much more satisfying to them than other forms of aggression.

A given frustration will instigate direct aggression. The next logical step is a consideration of the behavior to be expected when a strongly instigated act of direct aggression is prevented from occurring by a strong anticipation of punishment specific to that act. Since it is thus assumed that the act of direct aggression is strongly instigated, interference with this direct aggression constitutes in itself an additional frustration. And, according to the principles already stated, this additional frustration will be expected: (1) directly to instigate acts of aggression against the agent perceived to be responsible for the interference with the original aggression, and (2) indirectly to heighten the instigation to all other forms of aggression.

Obviously this vicious circle—frustration, aggression, interference with aggression, more frustration—tends to be repeated as long as successive acts of aggression suffer interference.[2] From this it follows that *the greater the degree of inhibition specific to a more direct act of aggression, the more probable will be the occurrence of less direct acts of aggression.*

When the argument is carried further, it is clear that, if all the acts of aggression directed at a given object are prevented, there will be a tendency for other acts of aggression, not directed at this object, to occur. A person may kick a chair instead of his enemy. In Freudian terminology, such

2. Whether the instigation to aggression will continue to mount until some act occurs or will tend to die down until the instigation to aggression finally disappears should depend upon exact quantitative relationships beyond the scope of the present discussion.

aggression is *displaced* from one object to another.[3] If, on the other hand, the prevention is specific to the type of act which would be direct aggression, there will be a tendency for other acts of different types to occur.[4] An individual may bring a lawsuit against his enemy instead of attempting to murder him; thus a *change in the form* of aggression may occur. Although these two kinds of change are not necessarily distinct functionally, they will be discussed separately.

DISPLACEMENT OF AGGRESSION

THE principle which has just been derived, that there should be a strong tendency for inhibited aggression to be displaced, is supported by a wide variety of observations from different fields of investigation. In turn, these observations are integrated and made more meaningful by the principle of displacement.

Superficially puzzling instances of behavior in which a tremendous amount of aggression suddenly explodes without apparent cause are often explicable on the basis of displaced aggression. A Southern girl whose life history was being studied had severely berated a porter who merely failed to have the exact change immediately on hand. Such behavior was exceedingly rare in this ordinarily mild-mannered girl. She herself was for some time most perplexed and dismayed by such a sudden, violent, and seemingly irrational outburst of temper. When questioned briefly, she revealed that on this

3. To be exact, one should distinguish between (a) that spread of aggression which is assumed to occur whether or not the direct aggression is inhibited, and (b) the displacement of aggression which, as has been deduced, should occur only when the more direct form of aggression is inhibited. Since few of the observations available to date have been so controlled that such a distinction can be made with any certainty, the term displacement will be used loosely here to cover both phenomena.

4. In the absence of specific data upon which to base principles that describe independently which of two types of action both directed at the same object will be the more direct form of aggression, the most direct form of aggression is dependently defined as the type of act which would occur in the complete absence of anticipation of punishment.

particular morning she had had a severely exasperating experience with her landlord, but had completely inhibited all aggressive tendencies toward him. As soon as this fact was called to her attention, she understood her own atypical anger toward the porter as displaced aggression.

On occasion, displaced aggression may have a somewhat happier fate and even serve socially approved ends. Lasswell (84) reports the case of a political reformer, part of whose zeal, the investigator believed, could be traced back definitely to basic hatreds against his father and brother. These hatreds were displaced to objects whose destruction was highly approved by the followers of the reformer. Some such displacements may be called sublimations.

A different type of evidence tending to support the principle of displacement is afforded by three simple exploratory experiments on aggression. In one of these, Miller and Davis (110) trained albino rats to commence striking one another, at the signal of a mild shock, in a manner similar to the way in which rats strike at one another when normally fighting. This behavior was reinforced by turning off the shock as soon as the rats were observed to strike one another vigorously. A small celluloid doll was then placed in the arena along with a pair of the trained rats; these particular animals tended to strike each other. Different animals, similarly trained, were placed *one at a time* in the same apparatus with the doll; these tended to strike the doll. A rat first attempted, in short, to strike the other animal, but when this was prevented by the absence of that animal it struck the doll.

In another study Miller and Bugelski (108) used an experimental situation to frustrate human subjects. The subjects were told that they were working in an experiment on coöperation and competition, and by proper urging they were instigated to do their very best. Then they were paired, one at a time, with a partner who, they thought, was just another subject but who was actually a confederate of the experimenters. During "coöperation" this partner caused the subjects to fail by bungling his part of all the coöperative tasks. During "competition" the partner caused the subjects to fail by succeeding well himself and making distracting remarks and invidious comparisons. A variety of other little annoyances, such as mispronouncing the subject's name, were also provided. Immediately after experiencing this frustrating situation the subjects tended to rate their friends lower on a simple personality scale than did control subjects who had not been subjected to these frustrations. Since the friends had not been present and could not possibly have been to blame for the frustrations which the subjects had just undergone, the more critical attitude of the subjects toward their friends may be taken as tentative evidence for the spread or displacement of aggression.

A third experiment, also by the same writers (109), took advantage of a frustrating situation in a natural setting. By chance it was known that, as part of a general testing program, boys at a camp were going to be forced to sacrifice a portion of their leisure activity in order to take long, dull examinations composed of questions which, on the whole, were too difficult for them to answer. At the outset the boys were relatively unaware of what was in store for them. Later it became obvious that the tests were running overtime and were preventing them from making the strongly instigated response of attending Bank Night at the local theatre; thus they were compelled to miss what they considered to be the most interesting event of the week. In order to exploit this situation, so loaded with frustrations, all of the boys were given brief attitude tests before and after the main examination. Half of them rated Mexicans before and Japanese after the main examination. The other half rated Japanese before and Mexicans afterwards. As would be expected, the attitude toward either set of foreigners was more unfavorable after the frustration of taking the examinations and missing Bank Night than before.

An apparently similar tendency is to be observed in the behavior of groups of Southern whites toward the Negro. The positive correlation between low economic indices and number of lynchings, cited in Chapter II, represents not only the variation in aggression with variation in strength of frustration but also the displacement of aggression to the Negroes. By no stretch of imagination could it be assumed that the lynched Negroes were the *source* of the frustration represented by low per acre value of cotton. That politicians as well as Negroes may be the target of displaced aggression is indicated by two studies which suggest that there is a greater tendency for rural districts to vote the incumbents out of office following years of poor rainfall than of good (10; 98). Since the politicians could not conceivably have been thought to be responsible for the rainfall, such a trend is perhaps an even more striking example of displacement than the well-known tendency for the public to vote against the party which was holding office at the onset of an economic depression. The processes involved in bringing about such displacements, to be sure, may actually be found to be quite complex.

CHANGE IN THE FORM OF AGGRESSION

In the foregoing examples, the chief emphasis has been placed upon the change in the object of aggression: rats struck at a doll when the partner they had been trained to fight was missing; a girl berated the porter instead of her landlord; strong but inhibited aggression against the father seemed to be at the root of a reformer's powerful instigation to organize political campaigns; boys missing Bank Night at the local theatre reacted unfavorably to far-away Japanese or

Mexicans; Southerners, frustrated by low values of the cotton crops, lynched Negroes; and citizens, frustrated by the
weather, voted politicians out of office.

It will be remembered, however, that, when anticipated
punishment inhibits direct aggression, changes may occur
not only in the *object* but also in the *form* of aggression. A
person restrained from actually shooting his enemy may
imagine that he is shooting him. A clear-cut example of the
indirect expression of aggression by the drawing of pictures
occurred in the experiment on sleep-deprivation by Sears,
Hovland, and Miller (143). Subjects were hired for the os-
tensible purpose of studying the influence of fatigue upon
simple physiological functions and were then prevented from
sleeping at all during one night. They were habitual smokers
but not allowed to smoke. For long periods of time they were
required to sit still without being allowed to amuse themselves by reading, talking, or playing games. They were led
to expect a meal toward morning and then prevented from
eating this meal by a "hitch" in the program. After being
subjected to these and other frustrations, they manifested
considerable aggression against the experimenters. But part
of this aggression, as was indicated by later reports, was not
expressed directly because of the social situation. Under
these circumstances one of the subjects produced two sheets
of drawings in which violent aggression was represented in
an unmistakable manner. Dismembered and disemboweled
bodies were shown in various grotesque positions, some
drowned, some hanging, some merely stabbed and bleeding,
but all portraying a shocking injury to the human body.
Furthermore, when the creator of these pictures was asked,
by another subject, who the people represented in the drawings were, he replied, "Psychologists!" And his fellow suf-
ferers were all obviously amused.

Humor and ridicule are other very common forms of aggressive behavior.[5] Anti-Roosevelt jokes would seem to be a current example. Viewing these jokes as an expression of aggression, one would expect to find them most popular among the members of the class that feels itself frustrated, either actually or potentially, by Roosevelt's program of social change. And it is in this very class that such jokes seem in general to be the most highly developed. In line with the principle that the instigation to indirect forms of aggression varies with the degree of interference with direct forms, it seems that in fascist countries anti-government jokes are most virulent. Since speechmaking and other more direct means of giving vent to aggression against the state are extremely limited, a joke whispered secretly about the dictators has tremendous punch.

The reading of horror stories appears to be still another of the manifold forms which the indirect expression of aggression can take. Here both the object and the form of the response of direct aggression are changed. If the reading of such stories is indeed an expression of aggression, it is not surprising that their popularity, relative to other types of stories in pulp magazines, seems to have increased markedly following the increase in the general level of frustration produced by the depression.[6]

SELF-AGGRESSION

A VARIETY of ways in which indirect forms of aggression may be expressed when direct forms are inhibited by anticipation of punishment has been considered; the individual, moreover, is also capable of injuring himself. Freud (46) has observed that certain melancholics persistently blame

5. That the individual at whom the humor is aimed perceives it as aggression has been demonstrated in an experiment by Wolff, Smith, and Murray (188).

6. An observation of Mr. Rogers Terrill, Associate Publisher of Popular Publications, Inc. Obviously it is difficult to be certain that the trend was the product of a single factor.

themselves for faults that are not at all characteristic of them but rather of certain loved ones in the immediate environment. Such observations have led Freud to conclude that these individuals are really complaining not about themselves but about the loved ones who often can be definitely proven to have frustrated the patient. It appears, then, that self-castigation may be a displaced form of inhibited direct aggression. Psychoanalysts have evidence seeming to indicate that not only verbal abuse but also physical injury and even neurotic symptoms of illness can be expressions of aggression directed toward the self.[7]

Perhaps the most dramatic form of self-aggression is suicide. Here the frustration, as in the case of the "rejected lover," for instance, is often very evident. It is interesting to note, in connection with the assumption that economic depressions increase the average level of frustration of the general population, that Thomas (170) has found the suicide rate to be higher during depression than prosperity.[8]

A shred of experimental evidence suggesting that much milder forms of self-aggression also may be correlated with frustration was secured in the experiment by Miller and Bugelski (108), in which a bogus partner for coöperation and competition conspired to frustrate the subjects. After their frustrating experiences, the subjects made many self-critical remarks. They also rated themselves lower on a simple personality scale than did control subjects who had not just been subjected to such frustration.

Cases of aggression turned against the self are apt not to be simple, since a certain amount of more or less direct aggression against others is likely to be involved. The hysteric with an ambivalent attitude of love and hate toward members of his family may have symptoms which injure them as well

7. In these cases the mechanism may be quite complex, involving factors such as introjection and guilt. For a more complete attempt to study the rôle of aggression in such behavior, see Horney (67) and Menninger (103).
8. For a more detailed analysis of this problem, see Zilboorg (189).

as himself. In American society suicide may harm others as well as the self. Among the Tikopia suicide is, according to Firth (43, p. 177), the son's method of revenge, a threat which constantly serves to prevent tyrannical fathers from becoming too unjust.

Illustrations have been presented indicating that aggression otherwise inhibited may be expressed against the self. From principles already stated, three deductions concerning such manifestations of aggression can be made:

1. It has been assumed that a frustration provides strongest instigation to aggression against the agent perceived to be the source of the frustration; therefore *instigation to self-aggression should be relatively stronger when the source of frustration is perceived to be the self than when it is perceived to be some external agent.*

2. It has been assumed that, when a given act of aggression suffers interference, this interference produces a further frustration which should tend to instigate new acts of aggression against the agent perceived to be responsible for this interference. Restraint by an external agent of an act of aggression, consequently, should instigate aggression against that agent; and self-restraint of an act of aggression should instigate aggression against the self. Therefore *there should be a greater tendency for inhibited direct aggression to be turned against the self when it is inhibited by the self than when it is inhibited by an external agent.*

3. Self-aggression is injurious to the self. Responses of self-aggression, therefore, inevitably carry along with themselves a certain amount of punishment. And it has been assumed that punishment tends to inhibit an act of aggression. From these two statements it follows that, *other conditions being constant, self-aggression should be a relatively non-preferred type of expression which will not occur unless other forms of expression are even more strongly inhibited.*

In general, these conclusions seem to agree with clinical experience, but opinion concerning them must be suspended until more specific evidence is available.

As a summary of the essential dynamics of the inhibition and displacement of aggression which may finally lead to self-aggression, the high lights of a case studied in detail by Mowrer (115) may be considered. A small boy in an institution displayed unusually strong aggression against adults. This took the form of biting, pinching, and hair-pulling. Under the severe discipline of the institution, this overt aggression was soon inhibited by expectation of punishment. Then the child began running after other children, biting them, pinching them, and pulling their hair. These manifestations of aggression were in turn eliminated, in fact so thoroughly that the child ceased biting altogether, even refusing to bite into solid food. Then the child commenced to pinch himself, bang his head, and to pull out his own hair. These actions were so injurious that he created bad sores on his body and two large bald spots on his head, and he finally had to be sent to another institution for treatment. Therapy consisted of removing frustrations, particularly those centering around toilet training and eating, and of attempting, by complete absence of threats, to remove the anticipations of punishment which were inhibiting direct aggression against adults. Under this treatment the child first expressed more aggression against adults and less against himself. Then, as the frustrations which seemed to have been the root of his trouble were lessened, his manifestations of aggression against adults began to weaken. The case appears to present a picture of frustration imposed by adults, aggression against adults, inhibition of this aggression and displacement of it to other children, inhibition of the aggression against other children and turning of it, still with much the same responses, against the self. During treatment this picture was reversed.

As aggression against adults became possible, self-aggression disappeared, and as frustrations were lessened, all aggression waned.[9]

CATHARSIS: EQUIVALENCE OF FORMS

It has been assumed that the inhibition of any act of aggression is a frustration which increases the instigation to aggression. Conversely, *the occurrence of any act of aggression is assumed to reduce the instigation to aggression.*[10] In psychoanalytic terminology, such a release is called *catharsis*.

When the little boy whose case has just been described became able to express more aggression against adults, his instigation to other forms of aggression seemed to be so reduced that self-aggression decreased markedly. Similar dynamics seem to be exhibited in a case, also from life-history material, in which a wife frustrated her husband by withdrawing money for household expenses from their savings account. The money was being saved slowly and arduously through the husband's rigorous self-denial of small luxuries. His wife's careless dependence on the account to tide her over when she ran out of her supposedly adequate household budget constituted a serious frustration to the husband's careful program of investment. Instead of being angry at

9. A somewhat different conception of the self-object relationship has been proposed by Rosenzweig (136) who has suggested that the reactions to frustration may conveniently be classified as "extrapunitive," "intropunitive," and "impunitive." These three types of response are assumed to represent the major dimensions to which any frustration-reaction may be allocated. Rosenzweig's "extrapunitive" type clearly corresponds to our overt object-directed aggression, and his "intropunitive" type to our self-aggression. The "impunitive" type does not correspond to any specific reaction pattern presented in the present book, but seems not only to involve change in both the object and the form of aggression but to be related to substitute response as well.

10. Presumably this reduction is more or less temporary and the instigation to aggression will build up again if the original frustration persists. Also the repetition of a mode of release may presumably produce learning of it. Throughout this hypothesis both the rôle of temporal factors and the influence of learning present problems acutely in need of detailed solution.

her, however, he berated himself. He said, "I don't blame you for not paying any attention to my wishes; they aren't worth worrying about. I'm no good to anybody anyway." Then he shut the door of his room and the wife heard him sobbing bitterly. Her abject apologies only brought more tears and self-recrimination. Nothing she could do was of any avail until finally she happened to say a few sharp words to him. This brought down an avalanche of vituperation on her head and afterwards the husband seemed to feel much better and could be comforted. Soon he cheerfully began to plan new ways in which the savings account could be restored.

In this instance aggression toward the self was evidently a characteristic direction for aggression to take. When a further frustration occurred in which the wife was clearly perceived as the frustrating agent, direct aggression was expressed. The "avalanche of vituperation" was presumably a much stronger aggression than would normally have been called forth by the "few sharp words" and was a response to the total instigation produced by the original frustration plus the later relatively mild one. This final aggression apparently served to reduce the strength of instigation to the self-aggression, since no further self-aggression occurred after the object-directed outburst.

One of the joint implications of the principles of catharsis and displacement is immediately obvious: *with the level of original frustration held roughly constant, there should be an inverse relationship between the occurrence of different forms of aggression.* This implication follows because, when any response of aggression is inhibited, its instigation should be displaced to the other responses of aggression; and, conversely, when any response of aggression is expressed, its cathartic effect should lessen the instigation to the other aggressive responses.

The clinical examples that have been cited as illustrations of catharsis also illustrate this principle of the inverse or reciprocal relationship between the expression of various forms of aggression. The folk observation that people who are quick to anger are likewise quick to recover is, if true, an illustration. The validity of the principle is further supported by two rather slender threads of experimental evidence. In the sleep-deprivation experiment (143), the subject who made the gory drawing was rated as expressing the most overt aggression. In a self-administered algesimeter test he pricked (injured) himself with the least pressure of any subject. By contrast, another subject, who seemed to be slightly nauseated by the experiment, was rated as expressing the least overt aggression and, in the algesimeter test, he inflicted more injurious pressure upon himself than did any of the other subjects. Since only six men participated in the experiment, the evidence is naturally merely suggestive, and not at all conclusive.[11] Further evidence was found in the experiment (108), already described, in which a bogus partner for coöperation and competition conspired to frustrate the subjects: there was a tendency for those subjects who gave their partner the lowest rating not to drop so markedly in their own ratings of themselves, the correlation between the ratings of partner and self being $-.3$ (S.E. $= \pm.1$).

The phenomena of catharsis and displacement seem to point to a functional unity in the variety of reactions to which the label of aggression has been attached in this presentation. To the extent that the type of functional unity which has been illustrated occurs generally and to the extent that it is strong enough to make the relationship between two so-called aggressive responses closer than that between one such response and many other presumably totally different types of

11. It appears that there are positive correlations between the occurrence of various forms of overt aggression and between various forms of non-overt aggression. The reciprocal relationship is probably between overt and non-overt on the one hand and between self-directed and object-directed on the other and may not appear at all if the amount of frustration is not held constant.

response, the suggested usage of the word aggression seems justified.[12] On the other hand, to the extent that the hypothesized functional unity is found, upon closer examination, to break down, the present use of the term "aggression" will have to be modified or abandoned.

SUMMARY

1. The strongest instigation aroused by a frustration is to acts of aggression directed against the agent perceived to be the source of the frustration, and progressively weaker instigations are aroused to progressively less direct acts of aggression.

2. The inhibition of acts of direct aggression is an additional frustration which instigates aggression against the agent perceived to be responsible for this inhibition and increases the instigation to other forms of aggression. There is, consequently, a strong tendency for inhibited aggression to be displaced to different objects and expressed in modified forms. Socially approved modifications are called sublimations.

3. Since self-punishment is necessarily involved, aggression turned against the self must overcome a certain amount of inhibition and therefore tends not to occur unless other forms of expression are even more strongly inhibited. If the amount of inhibition of various acts of aggression is held relatively constant, the tendency to self-aggression is stronger both when the individual believes himself, rather than an external agent, to be responsible for the original frustration and when direct aggression is restrained by the self rather than by an external agent.

4. The expression of any act of aggression is a catharsis that reduces the instigation to all other acts of aggression. From this and the principle of displacement it follows that,

12. *Cf.* the operational distinction between substitute response and aggression, p. 9, note 2.

with the level of original frustration held constant, there should be an inverse relationship between the expression of various forms of aggression.

5. It is the functional unity represented by the phenomena of catharsis and displacement that justifies attaching the label of aggression to the variety of responses considered in this theoretical presentation.

CHAPTER IV

SOCIALIZATION IN AMERICA

THIS chapter will deal first of all with the frustrations incident to growing up and living as an adult in American society. It will discuss also the aggressions instigated by these frustrations and the punishments with which society suppresses many direct forms of such aggression. Finally, it will analyze the social implications of the displacement of this aggression and will deal with the readiness to aggressive response manifested by adults.

Only the participant observer of social life can study these factors in full detail. The child learns the basic habits of its group from its parents. It receives its first rewards and frustrations in the family and not in the clinic or play group. It manifests its first aggression in reference to these same parents who not only give it care but also must force it, stage by stage, to abandon earlier goal-responses in order to develop the skills incident to living in its own group. With reference to this primary phase of socialization there are few data from the laboratory and even fewer materials of a natural-historical type. Since adequate documentation, let alone quantitative evaluation of the operating factors, is still difficult, the following exploratory account must suffice.[1]

1. The material in this chapter, therefore, must derive only minimal support from conventional child research. It depends chiefly on the following sources:

(a) Studies of adults. Here one must infer sources of frustration in childhood from observing the effects of childhood training on the character of older persons. The assumption is that the record of childhood experience is left in the habits of adults.

(b) An intensive, natural-historical study of the socialization of two children under four years of age. The material is recorded but not yet thoroughly analyzed or published.

(c) The studies of child analysts, largely reported in analytic formulae. These studies are of great value even though extensive observational ma-

The conception that childhood is a happy period has considerable currency in American society. As a result many workers underestimate the emotional costs of socialization. There is further the wish to teach the value of coöperative effort. This wish tends to direct attention away from the aggressive responses which just as inevitably attend social life. It is the purpose of this chapter to stress, and perhaps overstress, the frustrations incident to the acquisition of social habits. In doing so there is no intent to minimize the rewards involved in group living. It is clearly recognized that the purpose of group life is to increase satisfaction and to enable people to attain over the longest period of time the maximum number of goal-responses and to avert injury, delay, and death. Society could not exist without providing for its members the continuous and tremendous reinforcement of their basic needs. Frustration is, indeed, regularly used as a means of forcing the organism that enters a society to develop more complex modes of response which ultimately prove gratifying. Gratification and reinforcement are not, however, the factors selected for exposition in this book. The emphasis here will be on frustration and aggression as incidents of socialization, and it is to be regularly understood that the gratifying character of social life in America is thoroughly appreciated even though it is not continuously stressed. The object, in brief, is to systematize a new and a balancing point of view; i.e., to add to the widely held view that emphasizes the value of social life an equally vivid understanding of its costs.

PATTERNING OF FRUSTRATION IN CHILDREN

IF babies could talk they would tell their own stories of frustration: the continual modifications of behavior expected

terial is not given and even though they have been made on perhaps the most frustrated of children.

(*d*) Inferences that can be made from cultural studies which show the different problems set to children by different culture patterns.

from them, the arbitrary demands (from their point of view) made by adults, and the frequency with which established instrumental acts and goal-responses must be abandoned. By definition, such interference with established response-sequences is frustrating. Only detailed study can show how extraordinary are the achievements of children in our society in changing their behavior by the time they are six years old. Childhood is seen here as a period of persistent, forced, and sometimes violent, changes in habits.

It is to be remembered that it is the adults who organize a society and maintain its customary modes of action, including the techniques by which children are inducted into it. If technological changes impinge on a society, the adults rather than the children make the initial adjustments and change their behavior to meet the new situation. Eventually child training is also altered to be consistent with the new customs adopted by the adult world. It is the function of that part of the culture which deals with child training to prepare incoming group members for participation in social life as mature beings. When a child meets his culture, as Keller (77, p. 49) has shown, he meets an organized way of life, a set of problem-solutions which have served to adapt his group in some manner to its natural world. These solutions of adults are ready made and the child is compelled to learn and practise solutions to problems which he has not yet even encountered. The arbitrary character, from the child's standpoint, of the tasks set to it is determined by this forward-looking character of socialization; for example, the child is warned against strange bottles long before it has had the opportunity to sample bichloride of mercury; or the child is enjoined from exhibiting its bare body many years before the police have had a chance to pick it up for indecent exposure on Main Street.

Seen from the child's angle, the culture is presented in the form of a specific set of problems which must be solved. These tasks are actually learning situations or dilemmas in which the prescribed answer already exists. If the culture, for example, proposes oatmeal as a goal for hunger instigation, it is the child's business to eat it and like it and soon to give up its clamor for milk or ice cream. Other response-sequences have been in action, and they must be interrupted before new responses will be tried out and stabilized. It is one of the virtues of culture that the goals of action and very often the behavior sequences which lead to the goals are ready-made, so that in frustration situations with children random behavior is less necessary in establishing gratifying substitute responses than it is in other animals. During the time, however, between the interference with existing sequences and the learning of new, though already defined, substitute sequences, frustration supervenes even in those cases where the conditions of learning are ideal. It is evident from the above that only situations where the dilemmas, goals, and substitute responses are *patterned* are under discussion here. Such situations as weaning, cleanliness training, and control of aggression affect all children in American society and are regularly incident to group life. There are, in addition, problem situations, such as a rare illness in a child, which are not socially patterned but which occur and affect socialization by increasing frustration.

FEEDING

THE learning of culturally appointed habits begins early and runs through a series of stereotyped situations.[2] The timing of child feeding by arbitrary units usually begins immediately after birth; the particular times selected may be artificial from the standpoint of the child's hunger re-

2. It is possible that in passing over the birth situation one of the earliest frustrations is omitted, since birth may be an event interfering with responses previously characteristic of the child in its intra-uterine state.

sponses and thus interfere with strongly instigated response-sequences.[3]

The changes in pattern of response forced upon children in respect to the food habits of early life are obvious to all. The task is for the child to learn to like the food conventional in its group. Its first habits, however, are organized around sucking. In order that learning may proceed, these habits must be interrupted and the change to solid food must be made by the event of weaning.[4] Sucking behavior is not usually punished[5] in American society, although there are some societies in which it is.[6] The American method is to interfere with the response by withdrawing the bottle. The frustrating character of weaning can hardly be doubted, no matter by what method sucking is interrupted. Levy (88, pp. 99–101) indicates that the tendency to continue the original responses is strong, as is shown by the appearance of thumb-sucking, skin-sucking, sucking of strange objects from the environment, and the like. A ready substitute response is at hand, *viz.*, the chewing and eating of solid food and its type is designated by the society. Nansen (120, pp. 152–153) and Man (97, p. 81) have shown that where sucking the breast is neither punished nor extinguished it will continue for many years alongside the chewing and eating of solid food. Ameri-

3. The following discussion applies with most certainty to middle- and upper-class children. There is less certainty about the reactions of children from the lower-class groups. Parental attitudes toward sex and aggression may be different in the lower class about which so little is known.

4. Weaning is advised by the Children's Bureau publication, *Infant Care* (31, p. 61), at the age of seven or eight months and should be completed in a month or two. This remarkable bulletin has had a circulation of over ten million to mothers all over America.

5. It may well be that the distinction between reward and punishment will be replaced by a better one on closer analysis. It seems more useful for the present work to retain the concepts, however, and to use them in such a way that further analysis will not be precluded.

6. For example, Mead (102, p. 90) reports among Manʼians the use of lemon juice to paint the nipple; Junod (73, p. 60) describes the use of Jamaica pepper by the Ba Thonga; for the Nama Hottentot, Schapera (139, p. 868) indicates that bitter aloe is employed to smear the nipple in weaning the child.

can patterns, therefore, obviously make a point of interdict-
ing sucking responses and relentlessly pursuing the substitute responses, such as thumb-sucking (31, p. 49). Since
nursing involves both lip-mouth and hunger-appeasing goal-
responses, it is clear that our society provides only a partial
substitute for the whole nursing response. Appeasing hunger
is permitted after biting and chewing are learned, but for the
lip-mouth response component there is no ready substitute.

The frustrations incident to learning during the first year
of life may be great or small. It may be that time-scheduled
feeding does not accord with the natural hunger rhythms of
the child, in which case frustration supervenes. It may be
that arbitrarily dropping out the night feeding at a prescribed time imposes an additional frustration.[7] Any stomach
or intestinal complaint which necessitates the alteration of
nursing responses is bound to increase frustration, more especially since such complaints cannot be anticipated and the
modifications forced upon the child may be sudden and drastic.

The main contention here is that frustration results automatically during the change of food habits, that no one es-
capes frustration in this period, and that this situation is
engendered by our social patterns dealing with the learning
of new food habits.[8]

7. No position on the question of the proper mode of handling hunger instigation and the ensuing response-sequences is taken. This is in no sense a
challenge to the methods recommended by the Children's Bureau or pediat-
ric specialists, since it seems unlikely that the studies at present available
in this field are definitive. What seems certain is that the degree of frustration imposed is related to the time allowed for new learning, to the avail-
ability of a substitute response, and to the method which is employed of
removing an undesired response-sequence. Children might, for example, be
weaned by heavily rewarding other actions than sucking, or their sucking
might be simply extinguished by non-reward, or they might be punished for
carrying on sucking activity. It would seem that all of these methods are
used in American society to some degree.

8. Freud has viewed this period of life as one important in character
formation and has discovered in adult persons reactions which were based
upon the frustrating nature of such experience.

CULTURE DIFFERENCES

SOME of our[9] patterns of dealing with children frustrate them at points which are not paralleled in other societies, and the converse is also true. We do not limit freedom of movement as do some groups; for example, the Lepchas, described by Gorer (55, pp. 296–297), carry the child in a sling on its mother's back for most of its waking time during the first eighteen months of life. Nor do we inhibit crying *per se* by such punishment as pouring water down the nose of the child when it cries, as do the Crow (118, p. 275). Our children, therefore, escape these particular frustrating circumstances. Scientific innovation has also changed the patterned frustrations to which children are exposed. Since a disease in a nursing child might upset many of its goal-responses, it seems clear that the reduction in disease rates characteristic of recent years has greatly decreased frustration in this respect (157, p. 143). This is a case where cultural control of children's diseases (by inoculation and segregation) has tended to minimize frustration.

EXPLORATORY DOMINANCE

THE naturalistic observer of young children is impressed by the exploratory dominance behavior which they show with reference to the objects available in their milieu. Before the child can walk, this behavior may consist of putting any and all proffered objects in its mouth. This tendency must be interfered with in many cases, as when an object from which the paint may come off, a knife and the like are involved. After the child is mobile, its grasping, touching, and pulling gestures must be limited. It may not touch, for example, ash trays, cigarettes, stoves, radiators, glasses, or window shades; it must not beat or walk on polished surfaces, as on the piano

9. "Our" and "we" as used throughout this book refer invariably to our American society or to us as members of this society and never to the authors as a group.

or on the dining-room table. Initially the child fails constantly to discriminate between objects which may be pulled
or touched and those which may not, and its mastery responses must suffer interference. This very interference, of
course, is a means of enforcing proper discrimination.

Our society attempts to minimize the frustrating circumstances by providing substitute objects which may be thoroughly possessed, such as toys, balls, and old furniture. The
play room or "play pen" is also a solution here: either device
is frustrating in that it limits the child's motility, but satisfying in that all within the range of the room or pen may be
handled with a fine primitive frenzy. Limitations of motility
such as those imposed by the play pen may, however, be extremely frustrating, especially when important goal objects,
such as food or the parents, are observed outside the range
of motility. Crying, as a protest gesture, is frequently eliminated by disregarding it (31, p. 44), or by closing the door
on the child.

CLEANLINESS TRAINING

PARENTS will easily recognize the situation of toilet training
in the growing child as one in which response-sequences must
be changed in vital particulars. Peristaltic action and the ac-
cumulation of feces in the lower bowel originally release the
sphincter by reflex action, and excretion takes place in a
"natural sequence." This sequence must be altered by toilet
training. The effort is to insert other types of behavior between the appearance of bowel or bladder tension (the primary instigation) and the release of the anal or urethral
sphincter (the goal-response). This inserted behavior includes conventions concerning the time and place at which
excretion may occur. When this additional behavior is
learned, the child is said to be trained. This training, however, is no small job and apparently the interference with
the original response-sequence is exceedingly frustrating.

With very young children, the child may be put on a pot-chair and kept there for a specified period of time (31, p. 47). Its freedom to move is thus limited, and this limitation is resisted at first by the child in the form of cries and struggles. If the child's cries and struggles are disregarded, this constitutes an additional frustration. It may be important whether the parent holds the child on the chair or whether the chair itself is so arranged that the child cannot get out of it.

It is important also for the child to learn to loathe its excreta, since this loathing is a feature of the behavior of every well-trained adult. When children touch, smear, or smell their feces such training may begin. The parents may physically prevent such behavior, may punish the child, and will certainly voice disapproval of the behavior and make gestures which indicate revulsion. The child's excretory materials are interdicted as objects which it may touch or handle or eventually even refer to in ordinary social situations. The child's mastery responses to parts of its body are limited and interfered with by this training. Its anticipations of pleasurable stimulation from its parents may also be impaired and can only be reinstated when it has learned, with them, to detest and avoid its excrement. Freud (47, pp. 272–273) believes that the imposition of this learning is a vital frustration of the child's goal-responses of mastery and self-esteem.

The whipping of children for failures in sphincter control may be old-fashioned, but it undoubtedly exists widely in the population. Such whipping occurs when children excrete outside of the conventional place or when they exhibit unconventional behavior toward their excreta. The whipping not only interrupts the responses punished; it also interferes with the responses involved in the child's rapport with the parents. It is a double frustration. The withdrawal of customary rewards may also be used as a technique for enforcing cleanliness

training. The child gets no ice-cream cone if it wets its cloth-
ing. This too is frustrating.

Reward for success in cleanliness training is also commonly given. The child is praised for keeping its bed dry at
night, for example, and privileges may be given it, such as
an ice-cream cone or a piece of candy, on the days when it
has followed convention. It may be that learning is slower
when only the technique of rewarding desired behavior is followed and quicker where punishment is added to block the
existing response series. All in all, the imposition of cleanliness training takes some months of time and learning is slow.
This much has always been known, but what has not been
emphasized is that habits of reacting to other learning situations may be generated at the time that cleanliness training
is imposed. It is known that some children, after this experience, respond to any new attempt to get them to learn with
antagonism and bitterness (1, pp. 13–21). The two children
most carefully studied and reported upon for this period both
showed intense resistance and protest to training, no matter
what method was followed. There seems to be no way in which
a society can make cleanliness training painless. In the end,
there has been interference with original and natural responses and a new and time-consuming sequence has been inserted between instigation by bowel or bladder tension and
the goal-response of excretion. Though frustration must always occur in this connection, its exact strength undoubtedly
depends on the mode of training used and the time allowed
for new learning; ultimately, the frustrating circumstances
must tend to disappear since the new responses that are
learned also lead to adequate, though delayed, reduction of
bowel or bladder tension.

LESSENED DEPENDENCE OF THE CHILD

UNDER normal circumstances each child may also be said to
decrease steadily its dependence on its parents. It must learn

to walk where it has formerly been carried; and being carried is, of course, a *response* in this situation. It learns not to be picked up when it has experienced some small disaster. It must give up much of the cuddling, holding, and petting which is the prerogative of the smallest darling. Childish approximations of table manners and etiquette must be altered in favor of the customs preferred by adults. The child must learn to wait for its food, to keep its face clean, to submit to having its hair combed, to eat in the regular stages designated by our table techniques. At some time or another all of these lengthened sequences involve frustrations and elicit protest from the child. If the child has an infantile pattern of speech fixated by parental approval (because it was cute), it must learn to modify and abandon this mode in favor of the accepted phonemic structure. The time comes when the child is "too old" to cry as a means of protest in a frustrating situation, and this crying must be given up. Crying is sometimes punished and sometimes simply extinguished through non-reward. In this connection it is observed that vocalization of a protest type must give way to the more exact discriminations of speech. The child's demands for service, associated with its dependence, must become in general less urgent and masterful. It learns through the first four or five years the impossibility of achieving all of its ends immediately through stressing its helpless claims on others and also the degree to which it is enmeshed in a system that forces everyone to learn to play a relatively independent but coöperating rôle.

EARLY SEX BEHAVIOR

THERE is good ground for the presumption that masturbation behavior sets in automatically with small children as part of the body exploration of the child. When the prehending child first reaches its genital, it finds a highly sensitive organ whose titillation is gratifying. This manual stimulation tends to become fixed as a goal-response because of the high reward that ensues. It is, further, an act which can be carried out independently of other persons and therefore is in a class by itself among the things which small children can do. Since our society is unalterably opposed to masturbation in small children, this behavior must be abandoned. The modes of handling masturbation habits are varied. In the first place, the goal-response is prevented from occurring any more often than is necessary by extreme care not to stimulate the child unduly in washing its genital and by keeping the child clothed, so that it cannot reach its genital until several years of its life have passed. Indirect prohibitions are insisted upon, such as that the child must sleep with its hands outside the bed covers. In this case no reference need be made to masturbation as such and the prohibition appears an arbitrary one. In very small children punishment, such as slapping the hands, is frequently reverted to and the response-sequence is stopped by this intervention.

A technique of distraction is frequently advised and used, such as putting something else into the child's hand. This technique of removing the reward tends to prevent the fixation of the sequence. Verbal admonitions are utilized especially in later childhood, such as the threat (in the case of the male child) that the penis will be snipped off or that it will fall off if the child masturbates. The child is put in the dilemma of deciding whether it would rather retain the valuable organ in a physical sense and lose its use or use it and lose the organ.

Most adults who have been intimately studied show signs of inhibition in this sphere. A common case is the one in which verbal or other signs indicate the presence of genital instigation but the person makes no move to touch or rub his genital; the only inference is that the manipulatory response is inhibited.

The instigations and goal-responses related to masturbation are not ordinarily named for the child in our society. This failure to identify or to name the activity tends itself to exclude it from the series of response-sequences which may be practised. To give a neutral name to this behavior would perhaps indicate permission to indulge in it.

A minimum statement on this point would be that all children in the first year or two of life have learned and fixated to some degree a sequence of acts which involves the goal-response of sexual pleasure. In some cases this response-sequence may not be highly fixated and may be easily discouraged. In others it may be very well established and may therefore require extreme punishment to inhibit. A clear understanding of these alternative possibilities will throw light on the effect of masturbation taboos on subsequent habit formation. Prohibition of masturbation at a certain period of life may sometimes be generalized to all sexual behavior and so interfere with the possibility of adult marital adjustment of a person. It cannot be doubted that interference with the masturbation sequence is perceived as extremely frustrating and that it is in many cases a difficult habit to eliminate, no matter what rewards or punishments are connected with it. Mead (101, p. 136) has shown that the Samoans take a less emphatic position against masturbation than does American society with probable different results in adult character.

A particularly important achievement which has been discovered and stressed by Freud (47, pp. 174–177) is that of giving up the incipient erotic sequences which some children feel toward their parents in late childhood. At this stage of research on children it is possible only to indicate the factor of erotic attachment to parents; it is not possible to state its generality in the population. The cases in which such attachment is clearly demonstrated have been those of neurotic persons. The presence of attachment, however, may be much wider than in neurotic children since it is only on such children that we have adequate reports. Up to the fifth year of the child's life his habits have been built largely around the parents who have served as constant reinforcing agents. The parents come, therefore, in many cases to have a very high value to the child. It is not strange then that some children look to them also for aid in their emerging erotic life. Masturbation behavior, when it first appears, frequently involves open expectations of reward or coöperation from the parents; owing to our pervasive sex typing of behavior, these responses eventually are "directed toward" the parent of the opposite sex. These habits, which include phantasy components, are in part extinguished by the non-coöperation of parents, who themselves possess the inhibitions represented by the incest taboo. The child must learn to look elsewhere, or nowhere, or at least toward coöperation in a very remote future by somebody else. In the case of masturbation, as has been noted, the parents themselves, about whom the child may have phantasies while masturbating, may be the ones actually to punish the child for such behavior. When this overt and incipient sequence of responses toward the cross-sex parent has been eliminated by punishment or non-reward, the child is ready to establish relationships outside the family to a much more vital degree than theretofore. It is the testimony of the psychoanalysts (40, pp. 18–19) that the blocking of these erotically colored responses toward the parents is uniformly a source of frustration and often a crucial one. The bitterness which survives from it may color the attitudes of the person toward the parents for the rest of his life. The parents, of course, have no alternative except to impose this taboo. The discouragement of such erotic responses is a phase of the interference with responses of dependence upon the sociological parents.

SEX TYPING

It is essential that the social personality of each individual should turn out to match his sex in the biological sense; i.e., boys must have boys' habits and girls must have girls' habits. Sex typing endeavors to prepare children for their adult rôles as parents. Such typing, though obviously foreordained in a biological sense, is developed from the amorphous responses of the young child. Boys may learn, for instance, that they may not fight with their sisters but that they must fight with competitive age mates of the same sex unless they wish to be called sissies. Girls must learn that it is unladylike to climb trees even though boys may do so. Boys must learn that after a certain age period it is unmanly to play with dolls even though they formerly did so. Boys must learn that tears are not a proper response in a conflict situation, whereas girls are less pressed to give up this form of behavior. Girls may have to learn, for example, not to cross their legs in sitting down, whereas no such precautions are necessary for boys. The list could be extended indefinitely, but it is enough to indicate the changes in the response-sequences which are enforced under the heading of sex typing and which must be viewed as frustration to a small or a great degree. In some cases tendencies to revolt against the restrictions on older forms of behavior are still visible in adult persons.

AGE GRADING

Through the eyes of an anthropologist such as Linton (91, p. 429) one may observe that in our society age grading is quite marked. A child has a definite status and a corresponding rôle which defines what it may or may not do. Observation of children indicates that this rôle is not accepted by the child without opposition. It seems that with increasing verbal control of its surroundings, say in the period between three and a half and six years of age, the child gains a conception of its parents and of how they live their lives. In some way which is not well understood, it appears to begin to participate in all of their responses which are within its ability to grasp, and it begins to demand freedom to be "just like" the parents. It may want, for example, to be a parent itself, even though this is biologically as well as sociologically impossible. If the child has any conception of the sexual freedom which the parents enjoy it may also want the freedom to look or peek, to play in a sexual manner with other persons, to imitate coitus, and to use the terms relative to such acts. It is part of our conception of a child's rôle that all of such behavior must be inhibited.

A child may desire to stay up late, as late as the parents do, or to have the freedom to move about the house at any time of day or night as they do. If the parents wish any privacy, they cannot allow such freedom. When the child is put to bed, it must stay in bed. The child does not want to be left behind but would like to go just where the parents go. If told that it would find the occasion dull, it insists that it will be "good" or that there will be other children there to play with. Parents cannot consent to such behavior since our social patterns do not permit it (what would guests say if the small child were present at an evening party?). The child may wish to talk freely in a social situation and not only to have a regular "turn" with the parents but also to dominate the conversation if it chooses. It must learn, however, that it is "only a child," that "little people should be seen and not heard," and sometimes not very much seen either. The forms of this protest against age grading are altogether too numerous to recite in detail here, but they occur regularly in the growth of every child as verbal mastery of its world enables it to anticipate desired forms of experience. The great secondary reinforcing value of the mere presence of the parents obviously plays a rôle here. Children wish to be with their parents just because they are the ones who have so long rewarded, as well as frustrated, them. Now the child must learn both that it cannot do all the things that its parents do and that it must find ways of making life agreeable while it is alone with itself. This description is, of course, pertinent only to maturation of children in our own society.

SCHOOL FRUSTRATIONS

AFTER this long history of in-family frustrations, the child is sent to school. As everyone knows, this event involves a radical change of habits. The familiar setting and objects in the home, which have derived their value from the many gratifications experienced in the house, must be abandoned for a considerable part of the day. The preferred intimate relationship to the parents and all the responses based on it are inhibited, and a substitute person is presented in the form of the teacher. Many more rivals must be tolerated in the school than at home. The freedom of the child to practise its own satisfactory response-sequences must be abandoned to a considerable degree. The school offers a constant parade of new tasks to be faced and new words and skills to be acquired. The child must sit still for long periods of time when it was accustomed to move at will; it must not talk except in narrowly defined situations like recitation or in play periods. It must compete with other children, whatever its handicaps, for precedence in the school group. It may have to fight its way to school and home again—behavior sequences which have been more or less discouraged in the family itself. It seems likely that only active law enforcement by the community and complete parental solidarity with the school make it possible to keep the child in this new learning situation; he must be hemmed in and prevented from dashing out of the "field" by truant officers. Where such solidarity does not exist, for whatever reason, the child can scarcely be kept at the task of building a new set of goal-responses involving the school situation, since the frustration imposed upon it by interruption of its old ones is so strong. Erickson (38a) has shown clearly that this sequence occurs in the schools on the Siouan reservation.

ADOLESCENCE

ADOLESCENCE is known in our society as a period of increased aggressiveness and irritability on the part of children. This state of affairs is discussed in the next chapter of this book and will be given only passing consideration here. Masturbation responses apparently receive a renewed instigation and are met in various ways by the society, usually by threats and punishment. Instigators pressing toward heterosexual contact are also in operation and, because of our tight family structure, usually result in a transitory flare-up of the conflict over incest. Some children experience a renewed appearance of strong homosexual instigation and find it variously met by social patterns, though always inhibited in overt form. With sex instigation intensified, the play group rises in social significance and new learning must take place, especially with respect to personal appearance, manners, clothes, and formal behavior such as dancing. Habit orientation toward marriage and a career is in process of formation at the same time, since the two are closely joined to sex instigation. The final step from family dependence must be taken and the world is faced alone either at college or in marital and economic adjustments which begin in the late adolescent period.

FRUSTRATION IN ADULTHOOD

IT is probably true that the change of habits forced upon us is most frequent and radical in early childhood, but adulthood itself is not lacking in demands for readjustment. Marital adaptation requires the development of new skills such as sexual orientation toward another person and close communal living. The old demand for all of the advantages and none of the limitations of a course of action must be renounced. Limitation of attachment to persons other than the spouse is one such requirement of our monogamous pattern, and very few are the married who do not meet at least one other individual to whom they might also have been suitably adapted; many married persons find, or think they find, a considerable number. In this case, emergent sex responses are blocked, through internalized restraints and social fear. If, after the long delay of heterosexual response that is forced upon youthful persons in American society, marriage itself is not found gratifying, new disappointment and hostility will be the result. The gratifications of marriage are, of course, many and great if persons are so prepared as to make use of them.

An early demand of adulthood is the development of responses to instigation arising from requirements for a career. To some persons this means a postponement of marriage and renunciation of ease for many years while they acquire difficult skills. To others it means a career which is threatened constantly by loss of job, low income, fear of later insecurity, and feelings of inadequacy in the defined social status. For most people career adaptation requires foresight, renunciation of immediate spending and goal seeking, and constant prevision of a remote future. Old and persisting habits of dependence on other persons may have to be given up. Economic depressions throw millions out of work for indefinite periods and cast them into an inferior social group which must be supported by the community. For these people there is interference with vocational goal-responses. To the person in possession of elaborate skills, acquired with difficulty, this is a particularly bitter frustration.

For the many people in our society who are socially mobile, who wish to raise their status and income, there is a peculiar and chronic problem. Mobile persons must change their social habits according to models which they do not precisely see and understand, and there is no one to teach them. The groups to which they would like to belong generally react with resentment toward intruders and give the newcomers small opportunity to "learn to rise." This may result in a chronic anxiety concerning social status and in feelings of inferiority toward the better placed. When these mobility responses are interrupted permanently, they may instigate a blind and inexpressible resentment which colors the whole life of the person. Veblen (177, pp. 30–34, 102–114) has given a vivid picture of some of the frustrations occurring in the pursuit of high status; he has shown that there is a widespread pressure to raise status but that the room at the top of our social hierarchy is limited. Many must, therefore, fail.

The danger of war has recently become real to hundreds of millions of people, a danger not confined to the fighting forces. It cannot be denied by any adult in the modern world since war, like economic interdependence, has become worldwide. War involves interference with most of the satisfying responses in life both for the men who participate directly and the women who lose the men. Heterosexual sequences must largely be given up. The usual food satisfactions are interrupted, and the whole routine of daily life is replaced by one built upon quite another and sterner model. Since bystanders unaffected by war are becoming steadily fewer, the frustrations attending it are becoming mass frustrations.

To those most highly placed in American society the threat of revolution has become vivid since the World War was followed by a successful revolution in Russia and by several abortive attempts in Germany and Hungary. The specter of the vengeful underprivileged is a disquieting guest at the parleys and banquets of the rich. To the self-made rich this seems particularly unjust since they have endured so many sacrifices to gain their affluence and high status. The fear which the upper classes have that they may be forced to modify some of their goal-responses is a powerful current force in our society.

Natural catastrophes have largely been averted and minimized by the great efficiency of our society. Still floods do come and leave hundreds of thousands homeless, without food and exposed to disease. A ship sinks or an airplane crashes, and beloved persons are lost. A tornado sweeps across a Kansas plain and scatters the precious barn over a hundred acres of land, with discomfort and loss ensuing. Such events, resulting in interference with powerfully instigated goal-responses, necessitate painful readjustment.

Disease is a hazard hanging over everyone and experienced by most. It interferes with many of the on-going activities which bring satisfaction. It also cuts down income and the proportion of income that is available for other desired goal-responses. It is always at hand to frustrate.

For everyone in our society, the prospect of senescence and death is frustrating (67, p. 272). Knowledge of these events and anticipation of them is one of the features of our social orientation. Death is the final interruption of all responses and its anticipation is often attended by a feeling of futility and the sense of a life unlived. It is further made terrifying for many persons by being connected with ideas of punishment in the hereafter, ideas which are by no means always sloughed off even by those apparently most rational. "All men are mortal" carries an ominous undertone which makes it not only the major premise of a syllogism but a frustration as well.

The interference with aggressive sequences in American society will be discussed in the next section. In the meantime, it is apposite here that the interruption of aggressive responses is itself frustrating and often leaves the person in a condition of impotent rage. When aggressive responses are inhibited they constitute a permanent threat to personal integration; many of the meek are those who renounce all object-directed aggression in the anticipation that such responses once unleashed would go to disastrous lengths and hence bring about serious punishment. A chronic condition of helplessness, dependence, and frustration may be induced by the complete inhibition of overt aggressive responses. Individuals to whom this has happened are apparently fairly numerous and in many instances are neurotic. Such complete interference with all aggressive response is not the ideal pattern of our society, for individuals so limited become incapable of legitimate self-assertion and creative activity and therefore burdensome to the normal population.

THE REGULATION OF AGGRESSION

By the hypothesis, each of the frustrating circumstances already indicated leads to its separate flare-up of aggression.[10]

10. It seems worth while to put the statistical evidence on aggressive behavior at various periods of life along the time line here established and see whether other investigators have found aggressive behavior appearing where it would be expected. For example, is there more aggression appearing in school and clinic at the time of cleanliness training? The attempt is rendered difficult because of the different methods, terms, time periods, and conceptual frameworks of different studies.

Shirley (150, pp. 24–25) found that among twenty-five babies studied from birth to two years "irritability," as measured by "screaming" and "fussing" in test situations, reached a peak at the end of the second week, remained generally high during the first eight weeks, and diminished thereafter. It seems possible that "irritability" is correlated with the frustration incident to the first extra-uterine adjustments of the child. It is noteworthy that there is no heightened irritability exhibited at the time when the children were presumably being weaned. This may constitute negative evidence for the hypothesis that weaning is a relatively serious frustration.

Goodenough (54, pp. 70–76) reports a peak in frequency of anger outbursts for the age one to two among forty-five children (whose ages, when they were observed, ranged from seven months to seven years, ten months) followed by a rapid decrease in frequency until the ages six to seven years, ten months when there is a slight rise in the curve. These data may indicate aggression consequent on frustration in either weaning or cleanliness-training periods. The rise in frequency between the ages of six and eight may indicate hostility developed from school frustrations or from breaking emotional ties to the parents. Goodenough cites the corroborative evidence from Foster and Anderson (45, pp. 18–20), who, in summarizing one hundred case histories of children aged two to seven, describe a peak for temper tantrums among two-year-olds and a second rise among six-year-olds, the curve falling to its low point among the intermediate five-year-olds.

Murphy, Murphy, and Newcomb (119, pp. 390–397) and Stoddard and Wellman (158, pp. 359–361) discuss representative studies of the well-known period of "negativism" or "resistance" at the ages two to four, for which the peak is generally described as being at about age three. Bühler (27, p. 397) reports an analogous maximum for "exaggerated stubbornness," her data being taken from a clinic record of the visits of problem children.

The discussion will center on the forms of aggression appropriate to each type of frustration and on the manner in which aggressive responses are suppressed by surrogates of society.

Every member of a society learns by experience what categories of acts are defined by that society as aggressive. In their first learning individuals probably discover which of their acts are aggressive by the responses which others make to them. Aggressive acts tend to injure other persons and are commonly answered by counter-aggression on the part of such persons.

The necessity for suppression of aggressive sequences is clear to all who understand the nature of our interdependent society. Society may be said to have *learned* to suppress aggression in order to maintain coöperative life. Individual aggression puts sand in the gears and slows up the coöperative activity upon which all are dependent. Sumner (163, pp. 16–18) has long since noted the antagonistic undercurrent of social coöperation. One may paraphrase him by saying that coöperation is the lesser of the evils presented to social animals. Coöperative sequences, resulting in maintenance of life, are rewarded, whereas aggressive sequences are punished and eventually ended by death. Still, coöperative activity involves definite sacrifices and inconveniences to which the usual hostile response is made. Antagonism may be restrained by various devices in social living, but it is a factor to be steadily

This two-to-four-year peak is followed by a declining incidence until the ages ten to fourteen, at which point a second and lower peak appears with its high point at twelve to fourteen years. These data may be evidence for the rise in aggressive behavior which follows the frustration of cleanliness training, feeding problems, and inhibition of dominance tendencies. The heightened aggressiveness of children in the early age periods, as compared with the age group seven to ten, seems to be indicated.

The fact of senescence and the prospect of death is viewed here as frustrating. It may be that Cason's (30, pp. 82–84) data support this view. He found a peak for irritability (in terms of individuals' ratings of "annoyances") at the ages forty to sixty for a group ranging from ten years to old age.

taken into account. Control of aggression is especially crucial between the adults who make the society's living, repro-
duce it, and do its fighting. It is in order to form the characters of such adults that control of aggressive behavior must
be extended to the responses of children and must begin very
early. The anti-social adult is useless or dangerous to his
group. To fend off such dangerous characters we have fash-
ioned the whole system of regulatory behavior directed
against the aggressions of childhood.

There is so little knowledge of what average parents actually do in dealing with their children that no absolutely au-
thoritative account can be rendered of how the aggressive
responses of children are inhibited by punishment. Most parents tend to have some shame about their aggressions toward
children, and their reports tend to be self-protectively falsi-
fied. The forbidding atmosphere of our patriarchal family
bears directly on the disciplining of the children and on resistance to their aggressions. This atmosphere is expressed
in some of our precepts. It is necessary to "honor thy father
and thy mother." This commandment alone is a warrant for
a general aggressive parental program against the aggressive behavior of the child itself. One hears "I won't have a
saucy child around this house." Children are told "I couldn't
do that when I was your age"; and "spare the rod and spoil
the child" is less obsolete as an actual technique of child rear-
ing than might be supposed from the discussions of the most
enlightened. As will be shown, most of the aggressive actions
of the child are resisted at each developmental phase and the
mode of resistance is appropriate to the form in which the
child's hostility appears. Lewin (90, p. 616) has discussed
the "negative behavior" of the child as a reaction to parental
prohibitions.

There are two general methods of inhibiting aggression.
One is to put the aggressive response into a response-sequence
that leads to non-reward. "If you strike your little sister, you

can't have any dessert." This mode of treating aggression is often expressed as "withdrawal of love" or "privilege." The other mode of dealing with the child's aggression is to produce an inhibition of the aggressive response by punishment. The theme here is: "If you strike your little sister, I will strike you."

In the nursing period the neglect rather than punishment of certain specific aggressive responses seems to be a generally advised technique. Many parents do not reward crying, biting, scratching, writhing, jerking, and like types of behavior manifested by children. Spanking seems in general not to be used in opposing childish aggression in this early phase, and its absence corresponds to our appreciation of the physical helplessness of the child. If baby cries when he does not get his bottle as usual, we "pay no attention" to this cry and do not produce the bottle. Reactions of children which parents experience as aggressive may indeed be defined by yielding to protest behavior on the part of the child (31, pp. 44–45). It seems likely that in most cases there is no ground for long-standing resentment on the score of sucking deprivation since an adequate substitute response, eating, is at hand.

Against the first mastery tendencies of the child to touch, push, handle, beat, walk on, scratch, and the like, physical punishment in the form of slapping or spanking is often used. Aggressive perseveration in these acts, or attacks on the frustrators, are similarly punished. If the child is interned in a play pen, such mastery and aggressive responses become impossible with reference to socially forbidden objects. The effect of developing inhibition of its exploratory dominance and aggression by punishing or hampering the child through segregation is not yet understood.

In the case of toilet training, methods used to deal with aggressive behavior on the part of the child seem to be much more a standard matter. The child may be held on the pot-chair mechanically and its cries and struggles disregarded and thereby eliminated. A considerable percentage of parents use spanking after a failure on the part of the child to observe toilet conventions. Undoubtedly this spanking is used not only to punish and thereby inhibit the forbidden tendencies toward random elimination of the feces, but also to punish the child for protesting against cleanliness conventions altogether, i.e., for the implicit aggression involved. It may, for example, be spanked for struggling or crying after it has already been spanked for soiling or wetting. It may be spanked for running away from the chair. Another method is to frighten the child by scolding, where scolding behavior on the part of the parents is already recognized as a threat of punishment or of non-reward. If the child is able to and does verbalize its resentment, as by saying that the parents are "mean," it may be spanked or threatened with withdrawal of privilege. In any case, direct aggressive manifestations resulting from insistence that the child learn to be clean are met with a solid disciplinary front (i.e., punishment) by parents in our society. Children must learn both to be clean and to abandon overt resentment of this fact in all its forms. Since our conventions in respect to excretion provide adequate substitute responses for the original ones, there seems no reason why readiness to aggression should stem permanently from this sphere. In some cases, nevertheless, it appears to. That there is increased hostility at the time seems to be attested by various findings. Bühler (26, p. 397) has noted the frequency of "exaggerated stubbornness" between the ages of two and four years; Levy and Tulchin (89, p. 320) have noticed a peak of "complete resistance" (to authority) at the age of two and a half; Goodenough (54, pp. 171–173) has stressed the importance of "conflicts" between parents and children rising directly out of the cleanliness-training situation, in the second and third years of life.

Psychoanalysts (40, pp. 22–23) have found that the prohibition of masturbation in childhood is much more damaging than it looks to those who see it under the rubric of "habit training." The natural character and easy fixation of this behavior sequence have already been noted. In late childhood, furthermore, the habit of masturbation becomes involved both with the erotic wishes of the child toward others and with its self-esteem. Interference with this habit serves to limit the child's erotic behavior toward the parents and to lower its sense of self-mastery and control. When masturbation has once been prohibited, persistence in it becomes itself an act of defiance. Such defiance is met by still more vigorous threats and possibly punishment. Dangers to the body or mind of the child may be suggested, such as that he will not grow up or that he will become insane. Threats to cut off the penis are apparently quite common.[11] The punishing front of the parents is usually so severe that the child gives up the practice and forgets the painful circumstances, but does not give up its resentment; this resentment, in turn, is met with decisive opposition. Often the specific resentment is suffused in a general hostility toward the parents and family life, or appears in adulthood as a chronic suspicion of any who appear friendly toward the erotic wishes of the individual. The external threats become internalized (47, p. 175) and constitute a continuous frustration which results in a steady sequence of aggressive responses toward others. It must be noted that in contrast to weaning and cleanliness training no adequate substitute response is provided. It is not known in how many cases a pitched battle of this type occurs around the masturbation problem. Perhaps some children are less strongly instigated than others, or never fix the habit in the same way and therefore the battle is not necessary. In any case, the prohibition of masturbation is a crucial variable in social life, and its control, usually internalized, is a constant

11. A modern mother told one of the investigators that the problem of masturbation was easily handled in her young son. "All his father had to say was 'scissors.'"

source of aggressive responses; these responses may be expected to continue until a more adequate goal, i.e., a heterosexual partner, is available.

The parents are responsible for a whole series of frustrating events in the life of the child. These may occur in the case of food responses, excretory tendencies, mastery wishes, wishes to be grown up, masturbation or other behavior. The parents, in turn, according to the principles outlined in Chapter III, should be the immediate targets of the child's direct aggression. The occasion does not pass without direct attacks, such as striking or slapping at the grown-ups. Usually these are inhibited by anticipation of punishment. Some children relinquish them for the time only and go back to the attack later with actual hostile demonstrations against the parents. In early childhood, biting or scratching behavior may be reverted to. In this case, the child is usually pushed away so that it cannot injure the parent. Cases of slapping or even counter-biting are known. The presence of positive responses toward the parents is also a factor of importance. These normally become dominant over the hostile tendencies and exclude the latter from direct expression. But, according to hypothesis, there should be a strong tendency for inhibited direct aggression to be expressed in altered form or displaced to different objects. In many children a whole range of disguised forms of aggression toward the parents appear, such as shaming and frustrating of parents by school failure, cowardice, or exaggeration of illness. It will be suggested in the section on race prejudice that these aggressive responses toward beloved in-groupers are also frequently displaced and thereby permitted to run their course. It is also clear that some permissive outlets for aggression remain as in gossip toward mores-breakers, punishment of criminals, and situations in which it is beyond normal forbearance to inhibit aggression, as in the case of punishment of disobedient children by parents.

Aggressive responses between siblings are among the best-known problems which parents have. These obviously have two sources of instigation. The first is that one sibling frustrates another by taking its toys, tearing its books, receiving extreme preferential attention from the parents, and the like. Slapping, scratching, biting, crying, blaming, lying may all be manifestations of ensuing aggression. A second source of hostility between siblings is obviously that displaced from the inhibited direct aggression against the parents. Where parents can, they vigorously suppress quarreling between siblings by withdrawal of reward from the victor or frequently by physical punishment. To everyone who has grown up in a large family, the statement "You must not hurt your little brother or sister" has a familiar ring.

Aggressive responses generated by in-family frustration find a new target in the play group. The suppression of resentment is probably not quite so active here as in the family and is likely to occur only with genuinely damaging forms of hostility. In middle- and upper-class groups punishment of any aggression at all is more likely to occur than in lower-class groups. Still, competitive disagreements are expected among playmates, and there is some room for hostile expression. In addition to aggressions displaced from family members, frustrations imposed by the play situation lead directly to their own appropriate retaliations. In the play group, hostile behavior toward girls by boys is most likely to be punished. In many families, particularly lower-class families, aggression toward other boys may actually be rewarded by parental approval, especially when it appears as legitimate self-defense. Indeed, parents who suppress the aggressive responses of their children too severely may find them incapable of honorable survival in a play group, or, for that matter, in later life.

The aggressiveness with which children meet many new frustrations imposed on them by the school régime can only be met by a united front of the school and the home. Tacks on seats, throwing spitballs, putting a toad in teacher's desk, singing saucy songs about teacher are all familiar examples of this aggression. The refusal to accept the learning situation defined in the school must be suppressed if children are to be prepared for adult life; the teacher and the classroom rules she imposes may not be defied, and the child must not play truant. Wickman (184, pp. 123–128) compared the ratings of 511 teachers with those of 30 mental hygienists on the relative seriousness of behavior problems in school children. In general, the former in contrast with the latter rated as most serious those types of behavior which brought children aggressively in conflict with the mores of society and school. Punishment is directly inflicted by the school in terms of extra tasks, ridicule, and admonition. In the case of truancy, special officers may round the child up and bring it back against its will. Coöperative parents will punish the child at home by any of the familiar means if they hear of insubordination at school. "You can't listen to the radio until you get your home work finished." Here the parents lend their authority to a social institution to coerce the child into absolute acceptance.

The usual disapproval, admonitions, and withdrawal of privilege come forward again in adolescence to meet the increased hostilities of the child. Demands for new forms of expression, such as staying out late or using the car, are met by counter-insistence by the parents on the dutiful aspects of life. There is always the statement "I won't have any child around my house who does not behave himself, go to school, and keep away from bad company."

The sources of frustration in adult life are many, as has already been shown. All adult individuals have faced some or all of the frustrations listed and tended to react to some degree with aggression. Some persons react more readily with more powerful aggressive responses than do others. There

are many factors in adult life which tend to limit such aggressive expression. In the case of groups of adults taken
collectively, as in the nation, there is, of course, the fear of
counter-aggression, i.e., warfare. It is clear that this threat
hangs over all modern states and over all the men and women
who comprise them and is a potential punishment for collective aggressions on their part. It is also true, of course, that
this threat serves as a justification of preparation for warfare at the same time. Still and all, the threat of reprisal by
an enemy state undoubtedly limits the dominance tendencies
of any individual state; were this not true, a great unifica-
tion of world culture by the extension of some one state
would probably occur quite rapidly.

Within any given state internal hostility to the symbols of
authority is a common feature of social life. It is manifested
alike by labor leaders and capitalists as well as by groups
which hope for revolutionary change. Occasionally it breaks
out in the form of riots or insubordinate behavior such as
that directed against the Prohibition Amendment. The existence of such hostility and the necessity for measures against
it is clearly recognized by the custodians of force within our
American society. An army "white paper" (174, p. 11),
which is a plan for army action in case of internal hostility
against the state, exists. This paper goes so far as to locate
boulevards in our great cities on which planes might conveniently be landed in case of insurrection. The armed forces of
the state hold a constant threat over the heads of those who
would alter our social system by violence.

The police are the domestic army which keeps civilian order. They control aggressions between fellow members of society over issues of property and sexual or prestige competition. The police are locally controlled and are useful against
individual aggressors rather than against mass uprisings.
With the aid of the courts and prisons they serve to isolate
violators of our mores. The persons so isolated suffer a

marked withdrawal of social esteem (difficulty of getting jobs after release because of distrust) and are deprived also of the consolations of ordinary social life, such as freedom of movement and heterosexual gratification. The police, indeed, replace the disciplinary action of the parents toward children. Direct threat of reprisal by other individuals serves to limit aggressive behavior in situations which the police cannot immediately reach. Individuals standing in line may fight directly for their right to a certain position and thereby prevent others from infringing on this right.

It is obvious that not all in-group aggression is prohibited. There are circumstances of unendurable provocation where even murder is sanctioned, as in the case of the "unwritten law." Aggression may also be allowed where it functions to maintain the mores, as in resistance to a criminal act or condemnation of vulgarity and obscenity. In general, however, the most violent aggressive acts are monopolized by the state.

Undoubtedly most powerful of the sanctions which are coercive against individual aggression, however instigated, are social scorn, derision, and withdrawal of contact with the aggressive person. Every person's life is lived with reference to an immediate group of intimates and these persons, by withdrawing their approval, can administer a severe punishment for aggression against the common code. The terms "sneak" or "thief" or "chiseler" are probably worth more to social order than the army and police together because they strike directly at the income and the self-esteem of the person and reduce the gains of gregarious living; the term "rat" to label a traitor has similar effect in anti-social in-groups such as gangs.

As a force in maintaining in-group taboos on aggression, the influence of "conscience" can hardly be overestimated. Conscience or internal inhibition is a relic of the prohibitions on aggressiveness which have been imposed in childhood. It is that force which enables a person to be "good" when he is by himself. It inhibits aggressive acts before they get started in overt form and sometimes even the verbal expression of the instigation to direct aggression. Conscience must be continuously reinforced by punishment of the types just listed; if it is not, it may gradually become ineffective and will free aggressive actions as it weakens. Conscience may thus be frustrating in two ways: it may operate either against original sequences aimed at goal-responses or at the aggressive sequences that supervene when the former are blocked.

READINESS TO AGGRESSION

THE discussion in this chapter has dealt almost exclusively with American society, with the sources of frustration and the nature of the aggressive responses which ensue, and the societal opposition to these aggressions. If a great variety of aggressive responses are denied free expression, one would expect that there would be constant instigation to other aggressive sequences. This seems in fact to be the case. It is to be noted that the suppression of aggression occurs within a peace area by what Sumner (163, p. 12) has called an "in-group." The behavior which is aggressive is defined by the culture of this in-group and each member thereof learns to identify aggressive acts. It is fundamental for societal survival that anti-social acts against in-group members such as family members, schoolmates, fellow citizens, the police, national leaders, and generals be largely inhibited.

There are, however, substitute targets toward which aggression can be displaced within our society. Examples of such targets for displaced aggression include the villains who are constantly presented to us in moving pictures and detective stories, minority groups such as the Jews or incoming foreigners, and race groups like the Negroes. "Fascists" or "Communists" are probably often hated to a degree disproportionate to their real danger to our system. A preliminary account of work carried on under Lewin (90, p. 19) bears directly on the issue of displacement. In two groups of children, one "autocratically" and the other "democratically" led, the children in the autocratic group showed much more in-group hostility. The inference would seem to be that the "autocrat" leader frustrated these American children and produced instigation to aggressive responses that they were afraid to express toward him. The result was displacement of aggression from the leader to other children in the group and the development of scapegoats.

In spite of police and soldiers aggressive behavior does actually occur in crimes and lynchings; it appears also in games where there is wide emphatic participation such as football or wrestling. In every self-defensive class or clique formation there is also opportunity for aggression toward those who do not belong but who would like to get in. Trials and punishments of criminals are often avidly followed and give opportunity for aggressive tendencies to function in showing hatred of crime and its perpetrators.

As a result of his life history any given person will carry into adult life a high or low ability to "tolerate" frustrations and will stand at some point on a dimension of "readiness to be aggressive" in frustration situations. Some people are quick to hate and each small provocation in adult life is welcomed as an opportunity to release a flood of aggressive responses. Others are slow to hate and find it easy to "wait" in frustration situations. Perhaps these latter are the ones whose experiences have led them to expect that the frustration of a particular goal-response will be followed in near succession by a gratifying substitute response series. Perhaps those who show the highest tendency to respond to any frustration with overt aggression are those who, on the basis of past experience, have not learned that gratifying alternative responses will ensue; or they may be suffering constantly from secret sources of severe frustration which summate with those whose origin is more readily observed. Those who are instantly ready to respond to any slight frustration or anticipation of frustration with extreme hostility form a considerable and important body of the population and give a hyperactive character to any social movements in which they participate. One may think of each nation as having a large number of individuals who are constantly in need of some person, some idea, or some group toward whom aggression may be expressed.

AGGRESSION AGAINST THE OUT-GROUP

As Sumner has shown, peace within the "we group" and hostility against the "others group" seem to be correlated factors. The suggestion is here that these factors are dynamically related and that aggressive responses are often merely displaced from in-group members and find substitute targets in the out-group, i.e., those "semi-human" or "non-human" individuals who do not share the same customs as we. This is a clear case of a displacement of an original in-group aggressive response.[12] Displacement of aggression to race groups or movie villains within a society is apparently not sufficient to produce a complete catharsis. The chronic burden of intra-group frustration is too great to make this possible. Instead, out-groupers are, as it were, blamed for the frustrations which are actually incident to group life; and a host of aggressive responses are displaced to them. Because the Italian internal economy is so poor, the argument would seem to run, Italian soldiers are justified in bombing civilians in Spanish cities. For the out-group to be a good scapegoat it must be so far removed from the in-group by differences in custom or feature that it will not be included effectively

12. In the year 1095, Pope Urban II said to the multitude at Clermont, France: "Let those who have formerly been accustomed to contend wickedly in private warfare against the faithful fight against the infidel. Let those who have hitherto been robbers now become soldiers. Let those who have formerly contended against their brothers and relatives fight against the barbarians as they ought" (135, p. 314 note).

within the scope of in-group taboos on aggression. Out-groupers may then be thought of merely as perennial frustrators, as traditional enemies and threats to the integrity of in-group life. Often, of course, they are such in reality; but they are invariably so represented in order to seem to justify the displacement of aggression to them.

In summary, then, the thesis is this: frustration is a constant feature of in-group life because of the necessity of interfering with existing goal-responses so that new ones may be learned. Once adult status is attained there is still frustration resulting from the physical nature of man, inadequacies in social techniques in managing the material world, and the inhibition of goal-responses which is necessitated by societal life. Most of the direct aggression which follows upon frustration must be blocked within the peace area. Opportunities for displacement and limited expression are available and are utilized, such as maintenance of order within the group or attacking some of the sources of frustration as by scientific research. There still remain, however, many instigations to aggressive responses which are prohibited within the group and must be either directed toward the self at the price of great discomfort or displaced to groups of persons outside the society (49, pp. 85–92). This fact must be thoroughly understood if the organization of men into coöperative groups is to be realized. The plain implication is that one, though only one, of the conditions of avoiding war is to diminish intra-social frustration.

CHAPTER V

ADOLESCENCE

IN the preceding chapter it has been shown that socialization necessarily involves frustration largely due to the taboos and codes of conduct that exist in any society. The last important phase of maturation in the life of the individual and the last period of intensified socialization occurs at pubescence. It has been generally recognized that this period of adjustment is an especially critical one that produces many conflicts (141) and typical behavior patterns as a result of the efforts of adolescents to make adjustments to new physiological instigations and to learn the new habit patterns demanded by society. This interference with the redirection of drive-instigated behavior is presumed to be frustrating and hence an increase of aggression at this time is to be anticipated. It is the purpose of this chapter to examine some of the facts of pubescence, to attempt to analyze the main frustrating situations, and to describe some of the resulting aggressive behavior.

PHYSIOLOGICAL AND PHYSICAL CHANGES

IN order that the reader may be better oriented to the problem it is first necessary to review briefly the physiological and physical aspects of pubescence. Unfortunately the biological changes occurring at pubescence are not completely known. It is believed (6) that sometime between the ages of seven and fifteen, depending upon the individual, the pituitary gland becomes very active. The effects of secretions from this gland are at least twofold; both growth and the gonads are stimulated. The first effect is to increase the rate of growth; the gonads are later activated and, since the gonadal hormone counteracts the influence of the pituitary, the rate of growth

thereafter rapidly decelerates. These facts are important inasmuch as the rapid acceleration of growth occurs *before* the
sudden sexual maturation which is commonly understood to
represent the beginning of adolescence and inasmuch as at
this time the maximum rate of growth has been passed and
the annual increment of growth is already rapidly declining.

An analysis by Shuttleworth (151) of the annual increment of growth in individual girls has shown that the maximum rate of increase occurs about six months before menarche and that increments of growth have practically ceased
at two and one half years after menarche. Unpublished data
on boys by the same author reveal similar curves. As the average age of onset of pubescence is thirteen in girls (9) and
fourteen in boys (32), it can be seen that both groups approximate their full stature, on an average, at sixteen and
seventeen years of age respectively. Longitudinal measure-
ments of other bodily structures, such as weight, iliac di-
ameter, chest breadth, and chest depth, show the same picture: they reach their maximum at approximately two and
one half years after pubescence. Accompanying the maturing
of gross bodily proportions are the appearance of secondary
sexual characteristics, adult distribution of hair, the enlarg-
ing of the breasts in the female, the deepening of the voice in
the male, and the increase in size of the organs of reproduc-
tion (6; 93).

But the most important and dramatic effect of the increased gonadal activity is the intensification of sex instigation. Although exact scientific studies of the overt sexual behavior of human beings are yet to be made, it has been fairly
well established from case histories, personal observations,
and mass questionnaire studies that at pubescence there is an
aroused sexual desire which is most satisfactorily relieved
through genital stimulation (187). Harvey (60), in summarizing the results of ten other investigators who used the
questionnaire method, finds that from 1 per cent to 30 per

cent of the men and 4 per cent of one group of the women had had heterosexual experience before the age of fifteen. Achilles (2) reports that 60 per cent of a group of men interviewed stated that they had a definite sexual desire at the age of fifteen.

Recent investigations, moreover, have demonstrated that at pubescence there is a great increase in the output of sex hormone.[1] What part the specific hormones play is still conjectural, although there can be little doubt that the gonads provide an important source for the sex drive. Within the last few years synthetic male hormone has been injected into castrated animals and humans and has produced characteristic sexual behavior and feelings (112; 155). If the sex hormones are essential factors in sexual instigation, as these studies seem to indicate, then an increase in the amount of hormones present in the organism at pubescence should result in a change of behavior. Psychological examinations of a number of pubescent and post-pubescent boys have revealed that the quantity of hormone output apparently had a significantly greater effect upon the interests, attitudes, and stimulus-susceptibility of the boys than did either chronological age or physical status (156). Other investigators (159) have found that in two groups of girls who were equated for age, one group being post-menarchal and the other pre-menarchal, the sexually mature group more nearly approached the adult norms of interests than did those who were sexually immature. This evidence indicates that the effect of the increased secretion of sex hormones at pubescence is to intensify sexual instigation and to change the individual's reaction tendencies.

CHANGES IN CAPACITY

NOT only is the youth of seventeen physically and sexually

1. Unpublished data from the Adolescent Study Unit, Yale University.

mature, but he has also acquired most of the capacities of an adult. Brooks states:

Narrow experiment and wide observation alike indicate that coming to manhood and womanhood normally involves that development of motor capacities by virtue of which the individual not only is stronger but also has greater effective endurance of effort than he ever had before. (24, p. 55)

Studies of special abilities have shown that simple reaction time is shortest in the late "teens" (12), that muscular coordination reaches its maximum efficiency between the ages of fifteen and nineteen (104), and complex voluntary reactions increase in function up to age eighteen and then diminish (104). Also, so far as one can tell from the standardized tests of intelligence, the average individual has reached his maximum intellectual growth by the fifteenth year (168; 172). In other words, the average person of fifteen has, by any accepted criterion, the capacities of an adult; he lacks only experience and training, but otherwise he is fully equipped to cope with his environment and to participate actively in the society of adults. One does not need to depend upon the results of psychological tests to reach this conclusion. It is necessary only to review the achievements of the many youths who through either chance or personal initiative have successfully taken their place in a competitive adult society (114). Within a relatively short time the individual emerges from a phase in which he is of necessity almost entirely dependent upon others for his existence into one in which he has attained his maximum efficiency. His desire to use his new capacities and to be accorded the adult status for which he now sees himself fitted is a second type of strengthened instigation.

SOURCES OF ADOLESCENT FRUSTRATION

It is possible that under ideal circumstances the new behavior patterns might be learned without producing a measurable amount of frustration. In certain primitive environments the reaching of adult status is recognized as soon as it is attained. The post-pubescent is tested to determine whether or not he is worthy of entering into the society of adults and, if he satisfactorily fulfills the requirements, he is accepted by his superiors as one of them (118). In American society, however, these newly acquired abilities are prevented from functioning. Although the individual is physiologically an adult, he is sociologically a child. This period is one of "detachment of the young person from family control and marked dependence upon his age-group before achieving the degree of individual independence in the making of decisions characteristic of adult status" (134, p. 82). He is expected to conform to the adult restrictions and mores, and yet he is allowed very few of the advantages and privileges which should accrue at maturity. His sphere of activity is circumscribed, his efforts to assert himself are suppressed, his possessions are definitely limited, his economic independence is not tolerated, his status as an adult is unrecognized, and many of the restrictions of his childhood remain in force. These restrictions will now be examined. Their merits or demerits will not be discussed nor will an attempt be made to determine their origin.

One of the strongest taboos in the American culture is on sexual activity. In forty-three states the young male is not allowed to marry without the consent of his parents (169) and yet "a heavy taboo supported by law and by both religious and popular sanctions, rests upon sexual relationships between persons who are not married" (94, p. 112). These restrictions are so strong that even the subject of sex usually is not openly discussed. In a recent study (11) it was found that only 33 per cent of the young men and 45 per cent of the young women interviewed had received sexual information from their parents. Davenport (33) reports that of 880 spontaneous questions asked by 160 young women in a training school for teachers "there was nearly 200 per cent more interest shown in the primitive and anti-social manifestations of sex than in the whole range of socially approved avenues through which the sexual interests of youth and age are supposed to find expression." How strong this aversion is to the reality of sex is exemplified in the following statement of a Middletown mother:

"I believe children ought to be taught such things. I'm not much for talking about them. I've never talked to my daughter at all, though I suppose she knows more than I think she does. She's the only one I've got and *I just can't bear to think of things like that in connection with her.* I guess I wouldn't even talk to her if she was going to be married. *I just couldn't.*" (94, p. 145; italics ours)

This statement is indicative of the horror which the subject of sex arouses in some people. Of the five behavior traits that teachers believed to represent in children "an extremely grave problem," three were of a sexual nature: heterosexual activity, masturbation, and obscene notes and talk (184).

The effectiveness of interference with the goal-responses of sex instigation is demonstrated by the fact that the ten investigators summarized by Harvey (60) found that only from 6 per cent to 59 per cent of the men and from 7 per cent to 35 per cent of the women who were questioned had experienced heterosexual experience before marriage. It can also be expected that many of those individuals who succeed in circumventing the interfering agents cannot find completely free expression of the drive due to the fear and guilt feelings which attend the breaking of the taboo.

The second important source of frustration in the post-pubescent arises from the fact that his status as an adult is not accepted. The lag between the time he acquires the capacities of an adult and the time when he is allowed to demonstrate his independence may be as long as six or seven years depending on the age at which he becomes pubescent. During this period the youth gives every indication of being strongly instigated to perform the varied goal-responses appropriate to his new capacities, but tends to find that these responses are interfered with by adult restrictions. Most of the restrictions placed upon the performance of these responses have their genesis in the economic structure of our society. The lack of opportunities for the youth to be gainfully employed, and thus become financially independent, prolongs the sociological status of childhood. The recent survey of the National Youth Commission (11) revealed that only a third of seventeen- and eighteen-year-olds who were out of school were employed full-time and over half of those employed were dissatisfied with their wages; thus: "It is apparent that the privilege of working for one's living is unequally distributed between youths and adults. Whatever the opportunity for employment may be, youth have not not been receiving a proportionate share" (129, pp. 23–24). The situation is so acute that it was found that in Maryland (11) 48 per cent of the young males and 40 per cent of the young females, even though married, were still living with their parents. And it is probably true of our entire society, as the Lynds found in Middletown, that "the traditional view that the dependence of the child carries with it the right and duty of parents to enforce 'discipline' and 'obedience' still prevails" (94, p. 142).

It is probable that this rôle of the parents results from their failure to perceive that the individual under their care has reached adult status. Then too, even after the post-pubescent is recognized as having attained adult capacities, the parents must learn the new habits of treating him as an adult instead of as a child. Many restrictions, moreover, serve the function of giving ego gratification to the parents: they want their child to be dependent upon them as long as possible; they want to make him conform to the approved ways of the group because they are afraid that in the eyes of their contemporaries he will not be socially acceptable (185) ; and many of them hope that through discipline and training he will be able to rise beyond their own social and economic level so that they may eventually identify themselves with his success.

The practice of treating the adolescent as a child is carried over into the state and federal statutes which determine the legal age requirements below which individuals cannot participate in certain activities (127, pp. 105–106). The vote is limited to adults of twenty-one years of age or older. Persons under sixteen cannot be employed in industrial work. Most states require that the individual be at least sixteen before he may obtain an automobile operator's license and eighteen before he can operate as a chauffeur. He is compelled to go to school until he is sixteen. He cannot buy cigarettes or a glass of beer before a certain age. Chronological age, however, as has been pointed out in the first part of this chapter, cannot always be used as a criterion of "fitness."

EVIDENCE OF ADOLESCENT FRUSTRATION

THE general nature of the restrictions that are imposed on the maturing human organism by an adult society has been presented. The fact that such restrictions are in force would not necessarily make a frustrating situation. The restrictions must act as interfering agents, as something that prevents the individual from carrying through his particular repertory of goal-responses. If adolescence is a period of heightened frustration resulting from interference with sex-instigated activities and from instigation to attain adult status, evidence of the existence of such instigation should be found in the expressed wants and wishes of individual adolescents. That such instigation is operative is evident from the following sources.

In the Maryland survey (11) three-fourths of the young people interviewed recognized that there was a basic problem confronting all youth. Of these, 57 per cent said that the problem was the lack of economic security and the next largest number, 11 per cent, thought that the basic problem was morals. Impatience with the lack of independence is dramatically exemplified by the statement of one youth as follows:

"Young people have had to do a great deal of thinking for and about themselves, so if older people would make a greater effort to consider and respect their opinions and ideas, instead of robbing them of self-confidence and killing ambition by constantly reminding them that they are 'too young' to know what they are talking about or too young for real responsibility, youth would be far better off than they are today." (11, p. 253)

This statement is an echo of the earlier finding of the Lynds (94, p. 144) who reported that 369 high-school boys and 415 high-school girls rated "spending time with children" first and "respecting children's opinions" second as the qualities they desired most in a father.

Jersawit (72), basing her opinions upon the results of discussions carried on over a number of years with adolescents, believes that there are two types of discontents: the first, "those conscious dissatisfactions which have to do largely with restraints, overprotection, and the parents' unwillingness to trust young people with responsibility," and secondly, "the less conscious but more significant resistances to subtle pressures which the young people themselves cannot define." Boder and Beach (16) who presented a questionnaire to thirty-six girls and thirty-eight boys between the ages of thirteen and seventeen also found that the largest number of demands upon parents were for confidence and companionship of parents and a greater amount of social freedom. Symonds presents unpublished data, reported by Shuttleworth (152), indicating that at fourteen years of age in males and twelve years of age in females there is a sharp increase in the intensity of problems that center around money and around love, courtship, and marriage. In another study of the life problems and interests of adolescents Symonds (167) reports that the top six problems in importance are: money, health, personal attractiveness, study habits, personal and moral habits, and a philosophy of life.

All of the above refer to the expressed desires of young people. Such findings are indicative of their rebellion against the censorship and petty restrictions imposed upon them by adults, of their strong desire to be accepted as mature people, and of their awareness of the fact that they are still treated in many respects as if they were children. This means that in American society, where direct expression of sex-instigated behavior has been punished from the day of birth and where the individual's economic dependence upon the family is greatly prolonged, the more strongly instigated goal-responses associated with the newly acquired capacities of the adolescent are inhibited and substitute responses must be formed. The frustration attending pubescence is, therefore, a joint product of changes in the instigations of the maturing individual and restrictions imposed by the particular society in which this maturation occurs.

ADOLESCENT AGGRESSION

There must be general agreement with the statement that there are behavior patterns peculiar to the post-pubescent in this culture (24; 64). Aside from heterosexual activities, all observers have commented upon the adolescent's impatience with restriction, independence of action, gregariousness, recklessness, irritability, day-dreaming, and the more serious forms of behavior found in some individuals such as running away and actual delinquency. It would be an impossible and foolhardy task to try to explain all those reactions that have been observed in the maturing human being. The preceding paragraphs have laid the foundation upon which an attempt will be made to analyze the basic types of behavior which should make their appearance as consequences of the frustrations adolescents must endure. Even in the most ideal situations analysis cannot be infallible. One can speak only in general terms, since there are as many individual differences as there are individuals. Whether or not the individual is frustrated and the degree of his frustration will be dependent upon many variables: the strength of instigation, the degree of interference with goal-responses, the opportunities for forming substitute responses, and the effectiveness of the substitute responses in reducing the strength of the original instigation. Many of these factors will be conditioned by the manner in which former behavior patterns have been treated by parents and society. A complete interpretation of the behavior resulting from the new sources of instigation at pubescence is not possible without the life history of the individual.

Soon after the increase in quantity of the sex hormone, generalized goal-directed activities may be assumed to appear first of all. These activities suffer interference and overt aggression follows against the interfering agent or his surrogate, either of whom is usually an adult in the position of authority over the post-pubescent. This generalized activity, resulting from gonadal instigation combined with frustration-induced instigation to aggression, leads to the formation of substitute responses by trial and error. The means to some of the substitute responses are offered by society to the post-pubescents and others are obtained by them through the acquirement of special skills. Once these substitute responses have occurred and have reduced the strength of the original instigation there is a tendency for these particular substitute responses to be fixated and used on subsequent occasions; as a result, the probability of occurrence of a frustrating situation is reduced. Accompanying the formation of satisfying substitute goal-responses to the new sources of instigation is a gradual decrease in interference from society; consequently, after the initial sharp rise in frustration there is a gradual decline. This decline will be accelerated with the appearance of substitute behavior which more nearly approaches the characteristics of the original goal-response and which will also tend to reduce the variety and number of other substitute responses.

What are the facts which lend support to the above theoretical considerations? Is adolescent behavior characteristically aggressive and is this aggression particularly prominent during the first stages of pubescence? Unfortunately a great deal of the available evidence is only inferential in nature, but there are a few studies which seem to substantiate this reasoning.

The clearest example of an initial increase of aggression, at the advent of puberty, with a subsequent gradual decrease, is given by Bühler (26). In a group of girls ranging from ages nine to seventeen the greatest percentage who expressed intense "negative feeling" toward their families occurred among the thirteen-year-olds. The curve of percentage distribution of those who had bad social relations with their families accelerated at a regular rate from ages nine to thirteen and then decelerated at the same rate to age seventeen. Ackerson (3) reports that the peak of 4,454 cases brought before the Illinois Institute for Juvenile Research for personality and conduct problems is reached at fourteen years. There are no more cases of seventeen-year-olds than there are of five-year-olds.

There are other studies in which the *initial* increase of aggressive behavior at puberty is not shown because the information was obtained from subjects above fourteen years of age but which do indicate that there is a *decrease* in aggression after the onset of puberty. Bronner (23) has assembled a number of cases in which all the factors making for stability of conduct were presumably good before pubescence; but at sexual maturity these individuals appeared irritable, they ran away, and they demonstrated other anti-social traits. This behavior continued for a time and then normal behavior returned. In a study of delinquency by Healy and Bronner (62), in which the subjects were observed over a period of several years, it was found that there was a greater percentage of boys above fourteen years of age who showed improvement in behavior than there was in boys younger than fourteen. The explanation given for these findings is: "Independence gained through age, earning or the acquirement of status and other emancipations made possible by increasing age did play a part in a considerable number of cases" (62, p. 191).

Sollenberger (156) intimately observed the behavior of a group of boys between the ages of thirteen and sixteen over a period of six months and rated them as to their general aggressiveness. Only the behavior which was the result of some disciplinarian measure or some restriction placed upon the boy, which was directly observable, and which came under certain headings, was classified as aggressive. These headings were: various degrees of disobedience; emotional reactions (e.g., temper tantrums) ; and overt behavior such as physical violence or verbal abuse directed toward the disciplinarian, other people within the room, or inanimate objects. Assays for male hormone content in the urine were made independently immediately after the ratings were obtained. It was found that the relationship between hormone content and aggressiveness, expressed in a rank-order correlation, was —.94. In other words, those boys whose male hormone content was just beginning to increase—and from the assumptions made here this means an increase in sex instigation—were the most aggressive in the group and the boys who were further away from the time when this increase occurred were progressively less aggressive. There was no relationship between chronological age and aggressiveness.

The examples which have been listed as observed adolescent behavior may all be interpreted as direct aggression against the hampering restrictions of society. Also many forms of behavior described as adolescent are attempts on the part of the individuals to set up a society of their own wherein they assume the rôles denied them in adult society. The emergence of sororities, fraternities, and social clubs in high schools is evidence of this point. Bell, in the National Youth Commission Study, found that nearly 40 per cent of the school population belonged to one or more clubs and that "83 per cent of the club members preferred either much, or complete, independence from the guidance or dictation of adults" (11, pp. 170–171). The gang (173) is another example of the advantages that accrue by social grouping. As members of such a group, adolescents can display initiative, leadership, and the independent planning of activity. They mete out punishments, obtain in-group approbation, make laws, and perform many of the functions of a miniature society. An important by-product of the gang is, of course, the fact that its members gain strength through numbers to overcome actively the interference normally suffered from adult society. The compilation of collective experiences breaks down the inner barriers and allows freer expression of the various kinds of instigation.

Generally speaking, one is cognizant, within a particular society, that a specific type of behavior is aggressive. This is especially true of the reactions to the frustrations of efforts to attain adult status which are on a more conscious level than the reactions to the vague sex instigations and which take more easily observed forms of behavior. The post-pubescent, however, is more completely aware of the outward physical maturation than he is of the instigation that accompanies the gonadal change. He has had, in addition, more experience in observing just what advantages adult status has to offer. His goals are for this reason more sharply defined, and his activity toward these goals will be more direct. Barriers are broken through by downright disobedience or circumvented by bickering or arguing with those in authority.

The Lynds (94, p. 522) have found out that in Middletown the greatest sources of disagreement between high-school pupils and their parents centered about (1) the number of times the boys and girls went out on school nights, (2) their hours of retiring, (3) school grades, and (4) their use of the family automobile.

The most obvious form of aggression, overt behavior, is the one which is most strongly punished by society and therefore is the most strongly inhibited. Through years of training and discipline the individual has come to realize that transgressions against authority result in punishment; aggression therefore will often take a surreptitious form and will not be observed but can only be discovered from confessions of the individual. A young woman reports that as a child she had been trained to bathe every day and to make a complete change of underclothing and stockings every day. At pubescence she would go into the bathroom, run the water and splash the water with her foot without getting into it. She would then put on her soiled clothes and go down to the living room and meet the guests and curtsy as she had been trained to do, but all the time feeling a glow of independence because of the fact that she had broken the rules as to cleanliness.

DISPLACEMENT OF ADOLESCENT AGGRESSION

ANOTHER form of aggression which cannot be recognized as such unless all the aspects of the situation are known is that of displaced aggression. A case of delinquent behavior observed by Sollenberger (156) exemplifies the point. A clock that was admittedly stolen was found carefully hidden under the floor boards of a delinquent boy's room. He had no need for this clock since he already possessed one; this was an isolated case of stealing on his part. Questioning revealed the fact that he had apparently secreted the clock and had not used the act of stealing to gain prestige satisfaction in the eyes of his contemporaries; nor had the clock served any rational purpose. It was finally ascertained that the clock was stolen from a store several weeks before when the boy had been deprived of some privilege as a result of a minor misdemeanor. He said that he felt that his punishment was unfair and stated, "They wouldn't let me go swimming; so I stole the clock." It is clear that this delinquency represented retribution (aggression) in the form of violating *another* law when the boy did not have the daring to overcome the original restrictions placed upon him. But it is to be noted that the law that was finally broken was not imposed by the adult who produced the original interference.

Displaced aggression is also revealed in the espousal of "causes." Leal (85) reports that certain traits characteristic of physically mature boys and not in evidence among immature boys are impatience with restrictions, sympathy for the weak, and the desire to reform others. An analysis of the biographies and autobiographies of three prominent radicals has led Doob (36, pp. 258–259) to conclude "that an event had moved each one of them profoundly, . . . at the time they were all in the adolescent stage." Their revolts against the constituted authorities, identification with the weak and suppressed, and destructive behavior directed against the conservative elements in a society can all be interpreted as displaced aggression. These are rarely acts against the frustrating agent (the parents, school authorities, or the man who will not give them a job), but are directed toward some other form of authority.

There are many youths who are unable to obtain recognition and ego satisfaction either because the opportunities do not present themselves or because the conscience of the individual is so strong that he is unable to go against it and thereby suffers frustration through conflict. In these cases the aggression will take more serious forms such as are present in so-called psychopathic personalities. The aggressions may be overt and assume the form of fits of violence or attempts to escape from intolerable situations by running away; or they may be non-overt and result in mental disease and behavior disorders. Others whose overt aggressive responses have been unsuccessful will find relief in emphatic, non-overt experiences such as absorption in adventure stories and motion pictures, day-dreaming, romantic songs, and sex magazines. This type of activity at times becomes so gratifying that the individual who indulges in it never learns more rewarding responses and continues to live in a world within himself (27). In the majority of cases, however, either some overt aggression is expressed, appropriate substitute responses are learned and satisfactorily reduce the original instigation, or the factors which interfere with the responses disappear. More and more adults are becoming aware of the needs of the youth and are providing facilities wherein these needs may be expressed in a socially acceptable manner. For Middletown the Lynds remark:

The high school, with its athletics, clubs, sororities, and fraternities, dances and parties and other "extra curricular activities," is a fairly complete social cosmos in itself, and about this city within a city the social life of the intermediate generation centers. Here the social sifting devices of their elders—money, clothes, personal attractiveness, male physical prowess, exclusive clubs, elections to positions of leadership—are all for the first time set going. (94, p. 211)

CULTURAL NATURE OF ADOLESCENT BEHAVIOR

IT would be impossible to classify and explain all of the behavior which has been observed as typical of the post-pubescent. Here the point has simply been emphasized that in American society the process of becoming mature involves the inhibition and redirection of behavior resulting from several sources of instigation and that the predominant behavior symptoms of adolescence are aggression against the frustrating forces and substitute responses for those goal-responses which suffer interference. If adolescent behavior is a bio-socio-logical phenomenon and if its form is in part a product of the society in which physical maturation takes place, then these forms cannot be considered inevitable but must be looked upon in the same manner as certain neurotic behavior. Both are probably improper adjustments to the socializing processes of biological impulses. If the behavior patterns that appear at pubescence are the results of culture, therefore, it must follow, other things being equal, that in a society in which there is allowed relatively free expression of sex instigation that appears at maturation, the typical adolescent patterns will not manifest themselves. Those anthropologists who have been interested in adolescent behavior have reported that when these "ideal" conditions are present there is apparently little conflict at pubescence. Mead (101), who has conducted the most extensive studies of post-pubescent behavior in primitive societies, reports that in Samoa free expression of the sex drive is uninhibited and there is a marked reduction of adolescent conflict. Indirect evidence along the same line is obtained from Malinowski (96) who found that there is no neurotic behavior among the Trobriand Islanders as contrasted with the prevalence of such behavior among neighboring tribes where sexual activity is rigidly tabooed. Handy (58) observed that in the tribe of Ua Pou (Marquesas) the word "Ka'ioi" means "time of happiness" and refers to the period immediately succeeding pubescence. During this period the individuals have absolute freedom in which to satisfy their sexual desires. The members of a neighboring tribe restrict sexual activities and the word does not appear in their vocabulary. Williams (186) noted that the behavior of Soviet youths, who had been given emancipation from sexual restraints and had achieved responsibilities commensurate with their abilities, could in no way be classified as adolescent in terms of their social behavior.

Further evidence for the hypothesis that adolescent behavior is not an inevitable phenomenon but depends on the dynamic interaction of the personality in its own special environment may be found in the fact that so-called "typical adolescent traits" are *not* observed in many young adults. It is noticeable that numbers of post-pubescents adjust to the restrictions of our culture without the usual concomitant aggressive behavior. The picture, however, will not be completely clear until there is better understanding of the events which make it possible for these particular youths adequately to meet the frustrations accompanying the entrance into adulthood.

CHAPTER VI

CRIMINALITY

THE literature on the topic of criminality reveals a great diversity of factors which have been shown to correlate statistically with this phenomenon; there is, however, no generally accepted conceptual system of crime causation. Atomistic explanations stressing the etiological importance of now one isolated factor, now another, have repeatedly been put forward, but only to be sooner or later discredited. Many excellent empirical studies have been reported and a great many solid facts discovered, but the meaning of these facts remains largely to be determined. Criminology, as a science, seems still to be in that stage, which all sciences pass through, of collecting data and shuffling them about in more or less random fashion, without any well-defined natural categories into which they may be sorted and systematically dealt with. Until such categories have been established, scientific principles and laws can scarcely be expected to evolve; and the current view that "causes are multiple [and] grow out of the total situation" (162, p. vii) will continue to represent the ultimate in crime-causation theory. What would seem most urgently needed, therefore, in this field is the discovery of a few *common denominators* which will comprise as many of the isolated yet relevant factors as possible. As an exploratory step in this direction, two such common denominators are here proposed, the first of which is *frustration*, as previously defined in this book, and the second is what has been termed *anticipation of punishment*.[1]

1. The term "punishment" is here used to include not only the external infliction of injury but also the loss of accustomed gratifications, valued personal relationships, special privileges, etc. It is also important to keep in mind that punishment is no less a form of aggression than is crime. The fact that the latter is "anti-social" and the former is what may be called "pro-social," i.e., is aligned with and directed toward the enforcement and

The present chapter will be devoted to an attempt to determine how adequately these two concepts actually serve
their intended purpose. More specifically, the plan will be to
examine those measurable characteristics in which criminals
have been found to deviate significantly from the population
at large and to ascertain to what degree these deviations imply either higher-than-average frustration or lower-than-
average anticipation of punishment, the underlying assumption being that criminality, as a species of aggression,[2] will
vary positively with the former and negatively with the latter.

This approach, necessarily cross-sectional and statistical,
is fraught with many dangers, not the least of which in this
case is the inadequacy of the available data.[3] Many of the
sources which must be relied upon are old and especially unsatisfactory since they lack indices of reliability. Data reported by different investigators have often been selected according to widely divergent criteria; hence inter-comparison
and refined correlational treatment are frequently impossible. Many otherwise valuable findings that have been reported regarding criminals are rendered useless for present
purposes because of a lack of comparable observations for the

perpetuation of the mores of a group, does not alter the essentially aggressive character of both; crime and punishment both injure other persons and
therefore qualify, according to the definition employed in this study, as
forms of aggression. This tendency for aggression to be patterned along
opposing, i.e., socially approved and socially disapproved, lines has numerous implications for social theory which will be considered in detail at another time.

2. In the following pages an attempt will be made to show that criminal
behavior qualifies as aggression in the one respect that it is a reaction to
frustration; and the simple fact that a given type of behavior is forbidden
and is therefore termed criminal is almost axiomatic proof that it is directly
or indirectly hurtful to some one or more members of the group in which it
is forbidden. The problem of distinguishing between behavior which is "ac-
cidentally" injurious and behavior which is "intentionally" (criminally) injurious has already been dealt with and will not be reconsidered here.

3. References to criminological literature will necessarily be incomplete;
works selected for citation will be, in the main, either comprehensive sur-
veys and summaries or of such a character as to typify other representative
investigation on the same topic.

non-criminal population. Certain selective factors are also often operative, such as the fact that criminal statistics are derived in most instances from convicts (in prison or on parole) and do not, therefore, characterize offenders in general, including those who elude apprehension or else come to trial but are not convicted. In view of these and other limitations which might be enumerated, the following analysis is not to be regarded as in any sense definitive but rather as a means of stating and tentatively exploring the possibilities of an hypothesis and of posing some of its research implications.

(a) *Economic Status.* The most comprehensive survey of the relation between poverty and crime is that reported by Bonger (18, p. 440), who concluded from an analysis of data collected from various countries that "the poor supply a very great proportion of the convicts, in every case a greater proportion than they bear to the population in general, and the well-to-do form only a small part." Bonger found, for example, that in Italy during the years 1887–1889, 60 per cent of the population, classified as indigent or poor, contributed 88 per cent of the convicts. Other investigators[4] have studied this problem, but their findings have been in essential agreement with those of Bonger. To cite but one of the more recent studies, Shaw and McKay (148) found that in Chicago the coefficient of correlation by square-mile areas between delinquency rates and rates of financial aid to families by the United Charities and the Jewish Charities was +.74, between delinquency cases and dependency cases in the juvenile court was +.82, and between delinquency cases and mothers' pension cases was +.63.

It has sometimes been argued that poverty is correlated with crime, not because of any direct causal relationship, but because both phenomena are the common consequences of stupidity, laziness, or some similar trait. But the force of this contention is weakened by the observation, reported by vari-

4. Reviewed by Gillin (50).

ous writers (19; 51; 145), that criminality tends to decrease during periods of prosperity and to increase during depressions; it can scarcely be maintained that either stupidity or laziness likewise follows the economic cycle.

That poverty is a source of more or less constant frustration is indicated by the fact that when individuals have money their goal-responses are different from those which they manifest when they do not have it.[5] On the basis of assumptions stated elsewhere in this study, poverty would therefore be expected to lead, other factors being held constant, to an increase in criminality, as in fact appears to be the case.

But not only does low economic status lead to a heightened expectation of criminality because of higher-than-average frustration; it also tends to lower the inhibiting influence of anticipated punishment. Fines cannot be collected from penniless persons; and the threat of imprisonment has little deterring effect upon the individual who habitually experiences scarcely less deprivation outside of prison than he would inside. Human beings do not dread the loss of privileges and material advantages which they do not possess.

(b) *Vocational Status.* Bonger (18) has reported that unskilled male workers are implicated in all crimes (except "insult") more often in proportion to their incidence in the general population than are independent merchants, professional men, and "students and persons with income."[6] Fernald, Holmes, Hayes, and Dawley (41) found that 40.4 per cent of 517 female offenders studied in five New York State penal institutions had been engaged as domestic servants;

5. In modern civilized societies the total amount of frustration experienced on this score is probably greatly increased by advertising, by the movies, and perhaps to a less extent by the schools. Any agency which portrays other persons behaving differently from the way in which the mass of people are accustomed or financially able to behave and which gives the impression that anyone who does not behave in this different way is "missing something" can scarcely fail to have such an effect. Experienced poverty is obviously a function of one's relative as well as absolute level of achievement and possession.

6. See also Shield (149), Sullenger (161), and Gillin (50; 51).

about 24 per cent of the general female population was engaged in this type of work at the time this study was conducted. On the other hand, these writers found that only .8 per cent of their subjects had engaged in professional work, as against 8.0 per cent of the female population at large. Sutherland (165, p. 160) has reviewed the more recent evidence in this connection and concludes that "such comparisons show a disproportionately large representation in prisons from the unskilled and semi-skilled occupations, but the statistics are relatively unreliable and the comparisons are difficult. Furthermore, it is probable that arrest and convictions and commitments to prisons are distinctly biased against the unskilled and semi-skilled classes because of their helplessness to resist arrest and conviction."

That certain types of occupation are more arduous, disagreeable, or dangerous than others is obvious; by implication, persons who are forced into these intrinsically less desirable kinds of work will experience, other things being equal, a higher-than-average amount of frustration and will therefore show a heightened tendency toward criminality. However, since the various occupations also differ greatly in their remunerativeness and since no attempt has apparently ever been made to ascertain the criminality of groups in which vocational and economic status are independently controlled, substantiation of the foregoing deduction will have to wait upon further inquiry.

(c) *Educational Status*. The existence of an inverse relationship between criminality and educational achievement has long been suspected and has been substantiated by a variety of studies. Bonger (18) reported that of 1,209 juvenile delinquents in the English prisons during the years 1898–1899, only 9.1 per cent could be said to have had a "good education," but he gave no figures for the population at large with which this finding could be compared. Statistics published by the United States Government for the American prison population as of 1923 disclosed the following facts:

The figures . . . show, in general, a decidedly lower educational status for the prisoners than for the population as a whole. For example, the ratio of commitments per 100,000 of the adult population was 42.7 for the illiterate as against 27.3 for those able to read and write. Among the literate group the commitment ratio is highest (31.4) for those of only elementary school education and lowest (14.3) for prisoners who had had some college training. The commitment ratio is about three times as high for the illiterate as for the college group. (176, p. 19)

Brearley has reported that "for the 43 states for which homicide rates are available, the coefficient of correlation between the main rate of homicide, . . . and the percentage of illiteracy on January 1, 1920, was $+.658$ with a probable error of $+.06$" (21, p. 147). Sutherland has reviewed the more recent findings and states that "the conclusion is that crime decreases with the amount of formal education" (165, p. 177).[7]

Measures of educational achievement usually include or imply not only training in the technological sense, which tends to decrease frustration (through increased earning capacity), but moral training as well, which makes for increased anticipation of punishment. It is thus evident that the inverse correlation between criminality and educational achievement, as ordinarily judged, probably exists for two distinguishable reasons; but further research will be required to demonstrate the extent to which each is responsible for the observed relationship.

It seems evident that low educational achievement is not in itself frustrating. This is shown by the tenacity with which children normally resist the educational process. Deficient education is a source of frustration only at the adult level

7. *Cf.* also Glueck and Glueck (53), Pilcher (126), and Shield (149).

and then only to the extent that it leads to low income, inferior social status, or other conditions interfering with the performance of goal-responses. The fact that an education, once acquired, tends to reduce frustration is thus in no way inconsistent with the statement, stressed elsewhere in this study, that the acquisition of an education is always more or less frustrating.

(*d*) *Intelligence.* As Murchison (117, p. 28) has pointed out, there is a natural inclination to assume that wickedness and stupidity go hand in hand: "The author is not acquainted with any historical religion that has an intelligent and wise devil. Only the good are wise and intelligent. The devil and his followers are always foolish and idiotic."[8] Following an earlier period when feeblemindedness was regarded by many writers as virtually the exclusive explanation of criminality, the present consensus of opinion is that low intelligence is much less of a cause of crime than was formerly supposed. On the basis of an analysis of 350 reports on the subject of criminal intelligence, involving data accrued from the examination of approximately 175,000 individuals, Sutherland (165, p. 96) has shown that "the relationship between crime and feeblemindedness is, in general, comparatively slight. Certainly it is a much less important factor than age or sex. This does not, however, mean that it may not be a very important factor in individual cases."[9]

On the basis of the assumptions underlying the present analysis, it may seem surprising that stupidity is not correlated with criminality to a greater degree than the findings indicate. Not only would low intelligence seem likely to in-

8. "Comparing normal and criminal persons of the same age, Carrara found the *wisdom* tooth much more frequently present among normal persons. The percentage number of criminals showing no last molars is nearly quadruple that of normal individuals, according to Carrara's figures" (38, p. 65; italics added).

9. Doll (34) and Erickson (39) have argued for the existence of a somewhat closer relationship between intelligence and crime than Sutherland assumes.

crease the amount of frustration experienced by an individual; it would also be expected to diminish the effectiveness of the socializing forces in that it would imply a lowered capacity to appreciate the consequences of specific acts and a less keen anticipation of impending punishment. But since the normally intelligent man is instigated both by needs which are actually present and also, perhaps to an even greater extent, by anticipated wants, the person with blunted capacity for looking into the future is likely to have a relatively low level of aspiration and to find acceptable a life status which would be intolerable to a more intelligent person. The same limitation of intelligence which restricts an individual's learning and earning capacities may also make the ensuing low level of accomplishment far less frustrating than it would otherwise be.

(*e*) *Age*. Attention has repeatedly been called to the fact that crime is characteristically a youthful occupation (57; 126). Statistics show that delinquency as well as the more serious crimes increases among male offenders fairly steadily during adolescence, reaching a peak at the age of about twenty-five years, after which there is a negatively accelerated decline. The rate for all crimes for persons between twenty and twenty-four years of age is approximately five times as great as for persons over fifty; serious crimes are about fifteen times as frequent at the earlier ages (165). Fernald, Holmes, Hayes, and Dawley (41), in the study of delinquent women already cited, found that upon classifying their subjects according to four-year groups between seventeen and seventy-four years of age, the greatest number of offenders were between eighteen and twenty-two years.[10]

10. Shield (149) calls attention to the fact that, although the incidence of criminal behavior in general declines after a youthful peak occurring between the ages of fifteen and twenty-four, some types of crime, notably sex crimes and murder (as contrasted to property offenses), increase with age at least up to the forty-fifth year. Why this state of affairs should exist has apparently not been determined.

The fact that criminality reaches a peak during the twenties and thereafter declines has been explained in a variety of ways, none of which seems entirely satisfactory. It has been suggested, for example, that as human beings grow older they cease to commit crimes for the same reason that they cease to play strenuous games and drive automobiles recklessly, namely, because of a decline in physical vigor and emotional buoyancy. The hypothesis here offered is that the pattern of variation in criminality in relation to age reflects a corresponding pattern in the general level of frustration experienced by the average individual during his life cycle. With the approach of adulthood, the youth is forced to rely more and more upon his own resources; having enjoyed during earlier years a relatively sheltered existence, the young man or woman must sooner or later pass through a period of more or less profound readjustment on the road to self-sufficiency and independence. By the time the average man is twenty-five or thirty years old he has usually married, gained some degree of economic security, and established himself as a person of some importance in his community. From this time on, the discrepancy between his wants and his means of gratifying them normally lessens, having achieved by middle life a relatively stable equilibrium in this respect. Furthermore, as his possessions and means of securing gratification increase, man becomes increasingly conservative, having now much to lose through social retribution for wrongdoing. Thus, with advancing age, not only does man's general level of frustration tend to decrease but his responsiveness to the threat of punishment also increases, thereby providing discouragement against criminality from two sources.

On theoretical grounds, the relation of crime to the life history of women would be expected to follow a somewhat different course from the one it does in men. The fact that women usually marry men a few years their senior means that they achieve a comparable degree of economic security and impulse gratification correspondingly sooner than do men. One would consequently expect to find that the incidence of delinquency and crime among them would begin to diminish at an earlier age than it does in men, which, as the statistics already cited show, is actually the case. In societies in which woman's status depends largely on her physical attractiveness, it might also be expected that her tendencies toward criminality would be highest relatively late in life. The validity of this inference apparently cannot be established on the basis of data now available; but the fact that prison commitments for females is greatest in Finland between the ages of thirty-five and forty-five instead of during the twenties as in America shows that variations of this kind do occur (165).

(f) *Physical Size.* Smaller-than-average stature is quite generally regarded by men as a disadvantage and must be in some degree frustrating for a great many individuals. Although inferior size alone would not be expected to "produce" criminality in any given individual, it should show its influence statistically. Goring summarizes the findings of his monumental study of the physique of the English convict as follows:

To sum up: all English criminals, with the exception of those technically convicted of fraud, are markedly differentiated from the general population in stature and body-weight; in addition, offenders convicted of violence to the person are characterized by an average degree of strength and of constitutional soundness considerably above the average of other criminals, and of the law-abiding community; finally, thieves and burglars (who constitute, it must be borne in mind, 90 per cent of all criminals), and also incendiaries, as well as being inferior in stature and weight, are also, relatively to other criminals and the population at large, puny in their general bodily habit. (56, pp. 200–201)

Weidenshall (181) has likewise reported that the inmates

of an American female reformatory are shorter than the average working girl of fifteen.[11]

It may well be that in some cases the inferior stature of criminals is due to race, malnutrition reflecting low economic status, or some other factor which is independently correlated with criminality; to the extent that this is true, criminals are not criminal because they are undersized but they are both criminal and undersized for the same reason or reasons. However, it seems safe to predict that further research, in which this ambiguity is adequately controlled, will nevertheless reveal at least a slight connection between physical size and criminality, as originally postulated above.

The tendency for inferior stature to lead to increased criminality through a heightening of frustration may actually be lessened somewhat by the opposing tendency for smaller individuals to be less bold and more readily deterred by the prospect of retaliation. This supposition is supported by Goring's observation, already cited, that English criminals "convicted of violence . . . are characterized by an average degree of strength and of constitutional soundness considerably above the average of other criminals." However, the factor of size as a source of frustration is probably more important as a determiner of criminality than the influence of size upon the individual's reaction to the threat of punishment; for the latter is largely a product of childhood training, and during childhood the individual is always smaller than the surrounding adults, even though he be unusually large for his age.

A number of writers, notably Healy (61) and Slawson (154), have remarked upon the tendency for delinquent children to be either conspicuously larger or conspicuously smaller than their classmates and playfellows of the same

11. With the decline of the Italian school of "criminal anthropology," which held that crime was directly and more or less exclusively due to "congenital degeneracy," relatively little interest has been shown in the physique of criminals.

age. Marked aberration in either direction would be expected to be somewhat frustrating for children, although variation above the average would be expected to be less so than deviation below the average.

(*g*) *Personal Appearance and Physical Defects.* "I have wondered a great deal about the connection between crime and physical ugliness and deformity. That there is such a connection I have no faintest doubt" (122, p. 135).

There are probably two distinct reasons for the popular assumption that criminals differ from non-criminals in personal appearance, the one reason existing only in fancy, the other existing in fact. As Alexander and Staub (5) have shown, the villainy of the criminals in a given society regularly tends to be overestimated; for reasons which cannot be dealt with here, criminals are seen as personifications of all that is evil and odious and when so viewed are felt to deserve even worse treatment than is actually accorded them. They become scapegoats and whipping boys for the group as a whole and are commonly conceived as being in some vague sense not quite human. The atavistic theory of criminal types advanced by Lombroso and his school can now be seen in retrospect as primarily an attempt to give scientific status to this widespread social compulsion. Ellis (38) has reproduced thirty "authentic" pen sketches of "typical" criminals drawn by the governor of an English prison more than half a century ago; modern motion-picture portrayals of criminals seem to show that their appearance has not altered much in popular imagination during the interim.

Not only is there a tendency for criminals to be thought of as more repulsive-looking and misformed than they are, but there is also some evidence that they actually do deviate somewhat from the general run of individuals in the matter of personal appearance. It seems likely, on the basis of evidence reviewed by Ellis (38) at a time when the theory of atavistic criminal types was at its zenith of popularity, that an unusually large proportion of criminals have lower jaws which either recede or protrude to an excessive degree; and other peculiarities of physiognomy, such as overlarge or misshapen ears, were also reported as unusually common. That these findings were not entirely a product of the preconceptions of the time is indicated by the work of a number of recent investigators, such as Kilmer (78), for example, who reports that 44 per cent of a criminal group examined by him had "flap ears" as compared with 23 per cent of a non-criminal control group.[12] But it is not necessary to fall back upon Lombroso's theory of criminal degeneracy to explain the apparent connection between personal appearance and criminality. As various writers (122; 165) have pointed out, personal appearance is an important factor, particularly in women, in determining whether an individual will be able to gratify his desires and needs by legitimate, socially accepted methods or will have to resort to illegal procedures. It is easy to imagine the rebuffs and failures which offensive-looking individuals are likely to encounter in attempting to pursue many of the socially desirable walks of life and to understand why such individuals are prone to gravitate to the "underworld."

That the amount of frustration experienced by an individual is increased not only by unfortunate facial conformations and expressions, but also by bodily incapacities and defects, is obvious; that individuals who are so afflicted show an exaggerated tendency toward criminality is therefore not remarkable. Citing the Massachusetts Census of 1905, Sutherland (165, p. 84) says: "The number of lame, deformed, and maimed was 39 per 10,000 population of the state, while among the offenders it was 150; the number of deaf or dumb was 19 in the general population and 31 among offenders." The same census shows no greater incidence of blindness

12. Bridges (22) has likewise commented upon the relation of strabismus and certain other physical deformities to delinquency.

among delinquents and criminals than among the population at large; but blindness is so generally incapacitating and it so greatly reduces the individual's chances of successfully eluding apprehension that the fact that the blind are not more regularly deterred from criminal behavior than they actually are seems quite remarkable.

(*h*) *Health*. Since ill-health usually prevents the afflicted person from carrying out many goal-responses which seem important to him, it is unquestionably a source of serious frustration in the lives of a great many individuals; and the expectation would be, therefore, that such individuals would be represented in greater proportion among criminals than among the non-criminal population. Although Goring (56), Healy (61), Sullenger (162), and various other writers have interested themselves in ill-health as a factor in crime, the data necessary for arriving at any definite conclusion in this connection have apparently never been collected; in securing them care would have to be taken to distinguish between the effects of ill-health *per se* and of factors such as low economic status (resulting in undernourishment, exposure, and inadequate medical attention) which might be associated with it.

(*i*) *Hyperactivity*. It has been noted by numerous writers that delinquents and criminals are likely to be unusually restless and overactive. Post-encephalitic individuals have been found especially often to present such a picture and seem to find their way into court in disproportionately large numbers. Instead of supposing, however, that hyperactivity as such is a factor in the causation of misconduct, Sutherland (165, p. 99) has suggested that "the inferiority resulting from [post-encephalitic] lesions in the central nervous system lowers the status of the child, and the criticisms of parents and teachers when the child does not do as well as previously drive the child desperate."[13] Healy and Bronner have taken the position that the hyperactivity so often noted

13. *Cf*. Kahn and Cohen (74).

in delinquents who have never had encephalitis may be a consequence of fundamental maladjustment rather than a cause of it. They say:

A highly debatable question is whether or not such uninhibited behavior as we have just enumerated is caused by structural or functional peculiarities of the central nervous system, by obscure malfunctioning of other organs, or is the expression of emotional tensions occurring at even an early period of life as the result of situational experiences. . . . Evidently the question cannot be answered, but from some special observations we are forced to conclude that there is evidence that emotional thwartings and dissatisfactions, themselves dating back to very early years, may be the inciting cause of hyperactivity. (62, p. 45)

The primary purpose of calling attention to the frequently noted connection between criminality and hyperactivity is to show that even such an obscure relationship as this one need not be thought of as necessarily falling outside the scope of the present conception of criminality as a function of the two basic variables of frustration and anticipation of punishment.

(*j*) *Race and Nationality.* There is no serious contention among modern criminologists that individuals of any given race or nationality are *congenitally* either more or less prone to criminality than are those of any other group. But a mass of evidence has been accumulated to show that race, as a factor conditioning an individual's economic and social status in a given society, may play a very important rôle in this respect. American Indian men "were committed to prisons in 1923 3.1 times as frequently as American-born white men in proportion to the population, and Indian women 5.4 times as frequently as white women" (165, p. 112). Negro men in America are likewise arrested and committed to prison about three times as frequently as native-born white men in proportion to the population; and Negro women show an even higher incidence of criminality in proportion to white women.

That both the Indian and Negro groups in America experience a relatively great amount of frustration is commonly
acknowledged; and Dollard (35) has advanced reasons for
supposing that among the Negroes there is also a calculated
weakening (by the whites) of the socializing forces as far as
at least certain forms of criminality are concerned.

Certain immigrant groups, notably the Italian and the
Irish, show a somewhat higher crime rate than do native-born
Americans; but the factor of nationality shows its greatest
influence upon criminality in the offspring of the foreign-
born. "Special studies have indicated that the delinquency
rates of the second generation are comparatively low when
an immigrant group first settles in a community and increase
as contacts with the surrounding culture multiply. The rate
remains low in these foreign colonies which are comparatively
isolated from the surrounding culture. The rate is low in the
heart of the colony but increases on the borderlines where the
group comes into contact with other groups" (165, p. 114).[14]

It can scarcely be supposed that the economic status of the
offspring of the foreign-born is actually worse than that of
their parents or that they live at a really inferior level of
material comfort; but what seems to happen characteristically is that, as Americanization proceeds, an ever widening
discrepancy is created between existing living conditions and
the ideal standards of living which are created by American
schools, American advertising, and other powerful institutions, with a resulting increase of discontent. This heightening of frustration would be expected to make, therefore, for
increased criminality; but this is not the only way in which
the process works. Various writers have called attention to
the fact that the socializing influence of the family upon on-
coming generations breaks down in periods of transition from
one culture to another (22).[15] Parents stand for the old and

14. See also Beynon (15).
15. Ross (137) has taken the position, not easy to maintain, that economic
factors are alone operative in this connection.

the inadequate; and the normal process of identification with them, now recognized as of the greatest importance in character formation (4), occurs to a very incomplete and socially insufficient degree. The "clash of cultures," as Glueck and Glueck (53) have called it, is thus to be seen as not only increasing the amount of experienced frustration but as also seriously lessening one of the major socializing forces, *viz.*, anticipation of punishment.

(*k*) *Illegitimacy.* The earlier data on the relationship between criminality and illegitimacy of birth have been reviewed by Bonger, who found that in France, as an example, during the years 1890–1895, "a natural son runs twice as much danger of becoming a criminal as he would if legitimate, and that this danger is even four times as great in the case of a natural daughter" (18, p. 494). Of the various countries for which statistics were available, Italy alone showed no heightening of criminality as a function of illegitimacy. Sullenger has surveyed the more recent data and concludes that "children born out of wedlock have a much higher expectancy of delinquency than other children" (162, p. 29).

As in the case of race and nationality, illegitimacy as such can scarcely be supposed to have any bearing upon an individual's becoming or not becoming a criminal; but the consequences and implications of illegitimacy are such as to make for both increased frustration and lowered anticipation of punishment. Unwanted, neglected, and ostracized, the illegitimate child has a distinctly inferior chance of identifying with suitable persons and of gaining those internalized restraints which are essential to satisfactory character formation; and much the same forces also increase his difficulties in school and in earning a livelihood.[16] If every illegitimate child could be adopted into a satisfactory home, thereby insuring

16. Bridges (22) has given especial attention to the psychological effects of ostracism, humiliation, and other depressing experiences which illegitimate individuals are likely to encounter.

adequate socialization and no more than an average amount of frustration, the connection between illegitimacy and criminality should, according to the present hypothesis, be greatly lessened, if not completely eliminated.

(*l*) *Marital Status.* Perhaps the most dramatic demonstration of all of the rôle of frustration in the causation of criminality is afforded by the data concerning the marital status of criminals as compared with non-criminals. The following quotation from a United States Government bulletin dealing with the antecedents of American prison inmates as of 1920 shows this relationship with remarkable clarity:

A striking fact shown by the figures . . . is that, for both sexes and for all age groups for which significant comparisons can be made, the divorced population furnished a disproportionate number of prisoners. For divorced males the commitment ratio was 201.9 per 100,-000, or nearly three times the ratio of 72 for single males, and about six times the ratio for married and for widowed males. For divorced females the ratio of 24.1 per 100,000 was six times as large as the ratio of 4 for single, eight times the ratio for married, and ten times the ratio for the widowed. (176, pp. 23–24)[17]

That married persons enjoy, on the average, greater satisfaction of the important sexual and reproductive impulses than do unmarried persons is an assumption that can scarcely be questioned; and the data presented in the preceding quotation show the extent to which frustration in this sphere seems to increase the tendency toward criminality. Loss of accustomed satisfactions through divorce is exceptionally frustrating, and it is therefore not surprising that divorcees—who are often more or less chronically maladjusted in other ways —should show an unusually high crime rate. The only respect in which the facts are not immediately seen to fit the

17. Erickson (39), in his study of the intelligence of criminals, has likewise made the incidental observation that there is a higher-than-average incidence of single, separated, and divorced individuals among criminal populations ("for each level of intelligence") than in the population at large.

theory that increased frustration tends to increase criminality is that both men and women who have lost their mates *due to death* show an exceptionally low crime rate. That the loss of a husband or wife through death is ordinarily a source of serious frustration, i.e., disrupts many long-established and important habits, cannot be doubted.[18] Why, then, do persons who are thus affected not show an increase in outward aggression?

A perusal of anthropological literature reveals that if a people believe, as many primitive peoples do, that a person's death may be due to some agency outside himself (such as sorcery), individuals who are deprived of a loved (or useful) relative or friend show the clearest kind of aggressive behavior, relatively unmixed with anything resembling mourning, and set out to avenge the loss (frustration) which they have sustained.[19] On the other hand, in a culture such as our own, where death is seen as usually due to impersonal forces or is attributed to "destiny," to the "will of God," or to some other cause which man feels helpless or even fearful to combat, the resulting aggressive impulses apparently "turn inward" and give rise to the special experience of mourning or grief. In such a mood human beings are very little disposed to show criminal aggressiveness.

Frustration may also arise in the sex sphere, not only as a result of a person's being unmarried, divorced, or widowed, but also because of incompatibility between sex partners within marriage. Having found, in keeping with the United

18. The marriage relationship, like all other intimate human associations, is necessarily somewhat ambivalent. Every man and every woman presumably finds some features of married life frustrating. To the extent that this is true, every married person may be expected to find release from marriage —however satisfactory it may have been in general—something of a relief. But since the losses sustained through the death of a spouse ordinarily exceed the gains, the experience of frustration predominates over the gratification which is also present; and since the individual usually cannot bear to acknowledge this latter aspect of his reaction, the total psychological picture is still further complicated by marked guilt feelings.

19. Several good examples of this are given by Sumner and Keller (164).

States Government statistics already cited, that a greater percentage of male prisoners are unmarried or divorced than their non-criminal brothers,[20] Gillin also reports "greater disharmony between the [married] prisoners and their wives than between the brothers and their wives" (52, p. 208). Marital compatibility or harmony was judged not only on the basis of the responses obtained to direct questioning but was also inferred from the degree of similarity or dissimilarity of the background and cultural peculiarities of the husband and wife. Gillin concludes as follows:

Thus, on four points—economic status, education, nationality, and religion—the prisoners and their wives show greater differences [statistically significant] than the brothers and their wives. These findings suggest the possibility that these differences in background between the prisoners and their wives may account for the greater disharmony between prisoners and their wives than that found between brothers and their wives. (52, p. 211)

There is, of course, the logical possibility that some special type of childhood experience or an hereditary "taint" which makes for heightened criminality also creates an aversion to the married state and that the factor of frustration in the realm of sexual adjustment has no direct causal connection with criminality. The facts, however, do not seem to favor such an interpretation.

(*m*) *Sex Ratio.* Although the ratio of male and female criminals varies considerably in different countries—from 3:1 in Belgium to 22.5:1 in Finland—men are found consistently to be the more frequent offenders (18; 165). It is true that in certain respects men carry heavier social and economic responsibilities, yet it can hardly be supposed that the amount of frustration experienced by them is greater in the same proportion that their criminality exceeds that of women. Other considerations also have to be taken into ac-

20. *Cf.* Bonger (18), Fernald, Holmes, Hayes, and Dawley (41).

count. It has been suggested that women are naturally less prone to react aggressively than are men, but writers who have given the most careful attention to this question agree that such variations as exist between the sexes in this respect are largely socially determined. Physically smaller and weaker and periodically incapacitated during an important period of their lives by pregnancy and, to a less extent, by menstruation, women are taught to accept a protected albeit subservient position within the group. Lack of boldness and aggressiveness which would bring the greatest contempt upon a man is accepted as entirely natural and becoming in a woman. Bender, Kaiser, and Schilder have given especial attention to the reasons for greater criminality in men and conclude that the difference in the social expectations for men and women is of great importance in this connection; they say: "A fundamental causative factor seems to be our socially conditioned concepts regarding masculinity and femininity. Thus, passivity is felt to be feminine, aggressivity, masculine. A male needs to fight off any sense of femininity by physical activity—a masculine trait" (14, p. 408).[21]

Another important factor conditioning the incidence of criminality in men and women is the fact that when faced by adversity women can often find in the various forms of prostitution a solution to their problems that is not open to men. Although sometimes legally defined as a crime, prostitution is more likely to be treated as a form of immorality and tolerated as a necessary evil. Women who try to solve difficult life situations in this way are likely to lose social status, but with reasonable discretion they can usually avoid imprisonment. That prostitution probably saves a great many women from becoming criminals in the stricter sense of the term is indicated by a variety of facts. As women become less eco-

21. It is interesting to note the exaggerated masculinity affected by many criminals; the writers cited suggest that criminality in men is commonly due to reaction-formation against latent homosexuality and passivity.

nomically dependent upon men in a society, chastity seems to
be less highly valued and the need for prostitution accordingly diminishes; as this occurs and women are forced to turn
to other resources, their crime rate shows a decided tendency
to increase. Although reliable statistics are not as yet apparently available, this process has undoubtedly taken place in
the United States within recent decades (128; 161). Comparative statistics from other countries show that as men and
women approach a single standard of sexual morality, the
crime rate for the two sexes also becomes more nearly comparable; for example, in Denmark during the years 1876–
1885 the number of women convicted of crimes with respect
to the number of men was more than eight times as great as
in Algeria for the same period, in which country the standards of sexual conduct for men and women were far more
divergent than in Denmark (18). Statistics also show that,
whereas Negro women in America are committed to all types
of prisons seventeen times as frequently as white women, Negro men are committed only five times as frequently as white
men (165); and it is well known that Negro women are relatively little dependent economically upon Negro men and
that their standards of sexual conduct do not differ materi-
ally.[22]

Although the foregoing analysis is necessarily incomplete,
it will suffice to indicate the way in which the greater incidence of crime among men than among women can be brought
into line with the hypothesis that the two basic variables controlling criminality are frustration and the prospect of punishment in its varied guises.

(*n*) *Home Conditions.* So much attention has already been
given (22; 160) to the rôle of the home in determining the
criminality or non-criminality of the children reared therein
that this topic can be treated here somewhat summarily. The

22. This statement applies only to lower-class Negroes. Upper-class Negroes approximate white standards in this connection (35).

results of Glueck and Glueck (53), which are typical of those obtained by other investigators, show that of a thousand delinquent boys studied by them in Boston only 7.9 per cent had homes which were intact and afforded good supervision. In the remaining 92.1 per cent of the cases, one or both parents were gone from the home due to death, divorce, desertion, or imprisonment, or else the discipline and harmony of the home were impaired by incompatibility between parents or by the necessity for the mother to seek outside employment. These and similar unwholesome home conditions are likely to be associated with low economic status and privation of various kinds and thus to lead to an increase in the general level of frustration of the children affected by them; but probably more important is their effect upon the socialization of the developing individual. Superego or conscience is now believed to be established primarily through the existence of affectional bonds (i.e., expectations of reward and security) between a child and his parents; when these are weak or lacking or when parents are not fit models to pattern after, character formation does not proceed normally and the individual grows up deficient in those internalized restraints which, when combined with external social forces, ordinarily keep most individuals within the bounds of conventional conduct.

(*o*) *Neighborhood Conditions.* Despite the great importance of conditions within the home in determining the character development of children, the standards and practices of neighborhood contemporaries also have a significant influence. An isolated family usually encounters serious difficulty, at least in urban areas, in attempting to maintain for its children stronger anticipation of punishment than prevail in the rest of the neighborhood. Shaw and his fellow workers (148) have made a detailed study of the so-called "delinquency areas" in Chicago and have found that when families of relatively high standards are forced to move into demoralized neighborhoods, there is a definitely disintegrative effect upon the conduct of the younger members of the family. Playmates and school associates exercise a strong leveling influence which is sometimes so great as to be a source of considerable conflict for families with high standards of conduct but lacking sufficient income to avoid low-standard neighborhoods. Ridicule and disapproval from other children can either strengthen or weaken the socializing efforts of the home in respect to anticipation of punishment, and it is natural that an attempt should be made to keep both the home and the neighborhood ideals fairly comparable. Although socially inferior neighborhoods are also likely to be areas of deprivation and frustration, their main contribution to the ranks of criminality probably results from the fact that the extra-legal penalties for misconduct are less than in other communities.

(*p*) *Regional Conditions.* Numerous writers have remarked upon the higher crime rate in cities than in rural areas;[23] and one explanation which has frequently been offered is that the anonymity of the city offers greater opportunity for persons to commit crimes and avoid both legal and extra-legal punishment than exists in the country. Another factor which is less frequently taken into account is that in rural areas human relations are greatly simplified (57), man's major struggles being against nature instead of against other men; accordingly when man encounters frustration in a rural environment his aggressions are more likely to be directed against hostile environmental forces than toward other men, as occurs in city life; aggressions directed toward nature— such as imprecations and grumbling concerning the weather —are rarely regarded as criminal.[24] There seems to be no reliable way of determining whether the amount of frustra-

23. See the review by Ross (137).
24. It should also be recalled that, as previously noted (in Chapter III), farmers sometimes displace their aggressions inspired by frustrations due to crop failure to other men, such as politicians and Negroes.

tion experienced by city dwellers is also greater than that experienced by rural dwellers or whether the difference in the incidence of crime is largely dependent upon the factors just cited.

Brearley has shown that not only is the homicide rate a function of the absolute density of population in a given area, but that it is also dependent upon the rate at which the population is increasing. He says:

An indication that rapidly growing cities may expect an increase in homicide is shown by the data for Florida cities for the years 1920 to 1925. By the latter date the "Florida boom" in land values and population was well under way. In the six cities of the state there were 57 homicides in 1920 and 208 in 1925. An analysis of the individual cities shows even more clearly the effect of increasing numbers etc. (p. 149)

The data for counties, exclusive of cities of 10,000 or more, indicate the same tendency for growth of population to increase homicide [disproportionately to the absolute increase in population]. (21, p. 151)

This writer believes that "inadequate housing facilities, an increase of immigrants, and the social disorganization accompanying an influx of strangers" are the main reasons for the higher homicide rates in rapidly growing cities. These factors all clearly represent either frustrations or conditions conducive to frustration. The socializing forces are also undoubtedly weakened under these conditions: government regulatory facilities are often taxed to the limit and the greater mobility of a rapidly growing population also tends to weaken the force of custom and of community sanctions. Outsiders are ordinarily attracted to a given community in great numbers only when unusual economic gains are in prospect. The number of persons who look forward to profiting by such a situation is always greater than the number who actually realize their expectations, with consequent frustration of a fairly large number of individuals and an increase in criminal tendencies.

(*q*) *Alcoholism and Drug Addiction.* Alcohol has been called the superego solvent, and to the extent that it weakens internal restraints and also deadens anticipation of external punishment its use might be expected to correlate with criminality. On these grounds it has often been condemned as one of the major causes of crime, but actually it may be more of a substitute for than a cause of crime. Freud (49) has concluded that intoxication is one of man's trusted methods of rendering frustration tolerable ("drowning one's sorrows") ; if anticipation of punishment for misconduct is thereby weakened, so also is the frustration lessened. Sutherland has analyzed the statistics on crime and drunkenness in relation to the business cycle and has concluded that "In general these correlations are large enough and consistent enough to indicate that serious crimes increase in periods of depression, and that drunkenness increases in prosperity" (165, p. 161), thus lending support to the supposition, advanced by recent writers on the psychology of alcoholism (79; 105), that it is a reaction to frustration which is safer than crime and actually preferred by many individuals when the necessary money for indulging in it is available.

The bearing of drug addiction upon criminality seems to be not greatly different from that of alcoholism (81) and will not be given special consideration here.

(*r*) *Militarism and Moral Holidays.* Although the existing statistics are by no means complete, there is evidence that military life is likely to result in increased criminality. Bonger (18, p. 517) cites Hausner for the statement that during peacetime the criminality of soldiers "is 25 times as great as the criminality of civilians." Subjected to strict discipline, which may reactivate early childhood attitudes of resentment (116), and deprived of many normal opportunities for self-expression and impulse gratification, the soldier seems almost certain to find life in barracks unusually frustrating; the fact that formal penalties for misconduct are often exceptionally severe indicates that this frustration produces strong instigation to criminal aggression which requires strong restraints. Even so, these restraints do not seem capable of completely stemming the aggressive reactions to this state of affairs.

The incidence of criminality among soldiers during wartime is virtually impossible to determine. Standards of conduct are so disorganized and inverted that it is only by the most arbitrary definitions that anyone can say what is criminal and what is not. Behavior for which a civilian in peacetime would be severely punished may be encouraged during war, and normally innocuous actions may become highly reprehensible. That this confusion as to what punishments may be anticipated tends to have persisting effects upon soldiers is indicated by the fact that nations have always found it difficult to assimilate and re-socialize the men who return from wars. Corroborative of this common historical observation is the finding that in America in 1923 there was an unduly large proportion of ex-service men in prison (176).[25] This fact is probably to be explained not only as due to the disruption of traditional taboos and inhibitions but also, at least in part, as reflecting increased frustration through loss of jobs, disrupted personal relationships, or the like.[26]

All human societies set aside certain days or seasons during which behavior that is ordinarily forbidden is permitted; this arrangement, allowing periodic release of pent-up instigation, seems essential to the stability of any social group. It might be conjectured that this relaxation of moral vigilance and temporary lowering of standards would mean a reduction in behavior which would be called criminal, but this is

25. See also Erickson (39).
26. The fact that criminality among the civilian population of a warring country tends to decline (18) may be due either to displacement of aggression or to less systematic prosecution of crimes than normally occurs in peacetime.

not actually the case. Statistics show that a disproportionate number of crimes are committed on holidays (21) ; it is as if the forces of repression, once weakened, are likely to give way more or less completely. The increased number of arrests which are made on holidays has sometimes been attributed to the effect of heightened consumption of alcohol on these occasions, or to the fact that more persons are at leisure; but other considerations suggest that the mechanism already mentioned is probably also operative here.

(*s*) *Form of Government.* The total amount of frustration experienced by a given group is obviously influenced by the prevailing form of government. Other things being equal, an oppressive, inadequate government would be expected to result in increased criminality, and a just, efficient government would be expected to result in reduced criminality (25). A government, however, not only has the power to influence the amount of frustration experienced by the governed, but it also controls the severity of the punishment administered for aggressive reactions to the existing frustration. It is thus possible that a tyrannical government might greatly increase frustration and yet at the same time actually lower the incidence of criminality. This process can presumably go only so far without laying the basis for ultimate revolution or war. Obviously the problems involved here are complex and empirical data are difficult to obtain and interpret, as will be pointed out in Chapter VII.

(*t*) *Psychopathology.* By legal definition a criminal is a person who has committed a socially prohibited act and is judged to have been mentally and morally responsible at the time he committed it; such an offender is thus distinguished from a demonstrably insane offender and given somewhat different treatment from that which the latter would receive for objectively similar behavior. This fact accounts, at least in part, for the not very surprising finding that not more than 1 to 5 per cent of most prison and reformatory populations are psychotic in the traditionally accepted sense of the term. There is, nevertheless, a school of writers—notably, Alexander and Staub (5), Aichhorn (4), Lippman (92), and others—who believe that much, if not all, delinquent and criminal behavior is instigated by psychological mechanisms (mainly unconscious) which are basically similar to those believed to be operative in the neuroses and functional psychoses. In reading the works of the authors cited, the conviction cannot be escaped that they have often obtained exceptional insight in individual cases; but their findings do not justify the conclusion that all criminals are mentally disordered. Sutherland says:

> This preconception is shown in extreme form in the editorial in the *Journal of the American Medical Association,* Aug. 2, 1930, which was approved by the sub-committee on the medical aspects of crime, to the effect that a diagnosis of mental disease is "permissible even when the criminal has shown no evidence of mental disease other than his criminal behavior." A diagnosis of mental pathology assumes a criterion of the normal, and the normal in regard to thoughts, feelings, and sentiments is not stated in objective terms but is determined by the psychiatrist's preconceptions. (165, pp. 105–106)

More defensible than the position that mental abnormality causes criminality is the hypothesis that both of these phenomena are *alternative* reactions to frustration, the occurrence of the one or the other being determined by the entire structure of the individual's entire personality. According to this view, of two individuals who have experienced equal amounts of frustration, the one with a particular personality organization will be prone to react criminally, whereas the other with a different organization will be likely to show some form of psychopathology.

In the preceding pages an attempt has been made to marshal support for the hypothesis that all of the factors which have been found to be causally related to criminality derive this connection because of implying, directly or indirectly, on the part of the offending individual either higher-than-average frustration, lower-than-average anticipation of punishment, or both. This conclusion, once it has been arrived at, seems to sink almost to the level of a truism; but its validity has not always been so obvious. It must be remembered that a few decades ago the most widely accepted view of crime held that it was a mark of congenital degeneracy.

That criminality tends to vary inversely with anticipation of punishment is widely recognized by common sense. When crime increases there is a demand for more severe laws and for stricter law enforcement; and the home, school, church, and other character-forming institutions are looked at askance. This relation of the breakdown of the forces of social control to the incidence of crime in a given community has been formulated by Shaw as follows:

In short, with the process of growth of the city the invasion of residential communities by business and industry causes a disintegration of the community as a unit of social control. This disorganization is intensified by the influx of foreign national and racial groups whose old cultural and social controls break down in the new cultural and racial situation of the city. In this state of social disorganization, community resistance is low. Delinquent and criminal patterns arise and are transmitted socially just as any other cultural and social pattern is transmitted. In time these delinquent patterns may become dominant and shape the attitudes and behavior of persons living in the area. Thus the section becomes an area of delinquency. (147, pp. 205–206)[27]

Focusing attention upon the preëminent importance of the home as a socializing institution, Healy and Bronner say:

As we looked into the lives of these young people, it was clear, for one thing, that social restraints and inhibitions were in many in-

27. For a discussion of the relation of crime to radicalism (reform) and social change, see Katz and Schanck (76).

..... ces absent because of poor formation of what is so aptly termed an ego-ideal. There had been no strong emotional tie-up to anyone who presented a pattern of satisfactory social behavior. To put it in another way, the child had never had an affectional identification with one who seemed to him a good parent. The father or mother either had not played a rôle that was admired by the child or else on account of the lack of a deep love relationship was not accepted as an ideal. (62, p. 10)

If there is thus no novelty in the proposition that criminality varies inversely with the anticipation of punishment that is built up and reinforced through socialization, neither is there anything new in the suggestion that it varies positively with frustration. Bonger (18, p. 462) long ago cited the old Dutch proverb that "Happy people are not wicked" and pivoted almost the whole argument of his monumental book on the contention that criminality is a reflection of deprivations and dissatisfactions. This assertion, however, has certain discomforting implications and has not been as widely accepted as the logic of the situation would seem to warrant. As an illustration of this general tendency to neglect the importance and relevance of the frustration concept in the field of criminality, one finds Glueck and Glueck (53, p. 80) reporting that "on the whole we are dealing with parents and homes that in many respects must be characterized as unwholesome or underprivileged," but at the same time insisting that of the one thousand delinquent boys forming the basis of their study only 5 per cent evidenced marked "dissatisfactions" (p. 109).

Healy and Bronner have faced the problem of frustration in relation to delinquency more squarely and find that it is of major importance. They say:

It is through the lack of satisfying human relationships that feelings of inadequacy, deprivation, or thwarting are created. When these discomforts are powerfully experienced, the driving forces of wishes and desires naturally develop into urges for substitute satisfactions. When the young individual does not then find satisfactions enough in socially acceptable behavior (or does not develop inhibiting neurosis), he may find an alternative mode of self-expression through seizing upon the idea of delinquency. Thus delinquency really represents a portion of the stream of human activities which has a strong current behind it. Beginning with various types of discontents at frustration and continued as a drive for substitute satisfactions, the current has turbulently flowed along into the forms of self-expression that ideas of delinquency have suggested. (62, p. 201)

Although no claim to originality can be made in stressing the rôle of either anticipation of punishment or frustration as a major determinant of criminality, this phenomenon has not previously been seen and defined as a function of the dynamic interaction and balance existing between these two factors. Criminality is here viewed, not as a function of the absolute level of frustration nor of the absolute degree of anticipated punishment, but as a function of the discrepancy between the two. With a low degree of anticipated punishment, criminality does not result if frustration is also sufficiently low; likewise, given a high degree of frustration, criminality does not result if anticipation of punishment is sufficiently high. But when anticipation of punishment deviates in the downward direction and frustration deviates upward, the magnitude of the resulting discrepancy carries with it a correspondingly increasing expectancy of criminality.

CHAPTER VII

DEMOCRACY, FASCISM, AND COMMUNISM

THE frustrations involved in being and remaining socialized have been examined in Chapter IV and there it has been shown how the resulting aggression is regulated by the so-called mechanisms of social control. Here it is proposed to suggest very tentatively a concrete application of this psychological view of society to democracy, fascism, and communism. The analysis that follows cannot be considered adequate for all Americans, Germans, Italians, and Russians; rather it will seek to indicate the general structure of the society in which these people live and struggle, but only when that structure appears to lead to frustrations and aggressive behavior that are *distinctively* democratic, fascist, or communist.

The difficulties of describing the United States, Germany, Italy, and Russia in terms of the frustration-aggression hypothesis are frankly recognized. These particular nations, which have been selected because they epitomize different and competing political systems and philosophies, cannot be ordered very easily into simplified formulae: each has its own historical traditions, its own natural resources, its own aspirations, its distinctive complications. Each one, in short, is a society and no society can be squeezed into a few generalizations. Nowadays it is the fashion, moreover, to publish books on the subject of democracy, fascism, and communism (63; 66; 86; 175; 182), and certainly this chapter alone cannot be expected to present as many details and as much dogma as their pages contain.

To live in a democracy, furthermore, is to feel acquainted with the way such a society functions, but it is not always possible to achieve the "distance" essential for the valid analysis of every aspect of this society. To live in a democracy which is part of Western European culture is to experience some feeling of familiarity with Italy and Germany which are also part of that culture, but it is not always possible to avoid being blinded by the hostility that fascism deliberately creates within its opponents. To live in a democracy to which the writings of Marxians have diffused is to possess considerable insight into the theories guiding Russian communism, but it is not always possible to overlook a considerable gap between theory and practice, especially in that vast country. The bias and limitations of the present analysis, therefore, are thus apparent.

A final difficulty results from the caution with which the frustration-aggression hypothesis, being essentially psychological in nature, can be applied to sociological data. To claim, for example, that a given situation is frustrating, it is really necessary to be so well acquainted with the individuals concerned that goal-responses which have suffered interferences can be rather definitely identified. Intimate psychological information of this sort is lacking for all three of the political systems that are being considered. For this reason the alleged existence of frustration and the designation of aggression are purely inferential. The risk of making such inferences from statistics and secondary sources is being incurred in order to illustrate how democracy, fascism, and communism might be analyzed in terms of frustration and aggression: this psychological system is equipped, in short, to conceptualize sociological materials the very moment they yield psychological insights. Until more precise data are secured—if they ever can be secured—no valid quantitative comparison between the frustrations and gratifications characterizing democracy, fascism, and communism can be made; all that can and will be done is to show how the comparison could be made by means of this hypothesis.

SOCIALIZATION OF CHILDREN

In addition to the home, it is the formal system of education that is very influential in transmitting the social heritage. School children are frustrated as they are taught their social rôles and the ways in which they may express aggression. Graduates from democratic, fascist, and communist institutions, therefore, are different kinds of people and have differing expectations for the future.

In America the increased acceptance of the tenets of progressive education is an indication that American educators are inclined, whenever possible, to diminish the frustrations inherent in the classroom. Every convention of teachers, moreover, is troubled by the problem of the "how," i.e., the most effective techniques of teaching. Concerning the goal of American education there is no verbal agreement. Certain members of the staff of Teachers College in Columbia University, for example, devote a good deal of their time and their periodicals to debating whether children should be prepared for the status quo, for a new kind of collectivism, or for whatever society is in the process of being evolved. In practice, however, with the exception of a few courses in some of the institutions of higher learning, teachers either intentionally or unintentionally indoctrinate their pupils with what are vaguely called American ideals: America is the best country in the world, America gives everyone an opportunity to rise in the economic and social scale, Americans must be true to the principles of the Constitution. This indoctrination is seldom systematic in the fascist or communist sense and Americans, therefore, do not fit a completely stereotyped format. There is, furthermore, a contradiction between the ideal and the practice of American education: on the one hand the virtue of coöperation is stressed in the name of "service," "good conduct," or "character"; and on the other competition for grades is tolerated in all but the most "ad-

vanced" schools. Afterwards almost all adults praise the education they have received and claim that it has helped them
both economically and culturally (11, p. 82).

The ubiquitous youth organizations in Germany and Italy
demonstrate that Hitler and Mussolini are attempting to secure supporters by beginning to form them in the cradle.
German educators frown upon the progressive ideas that
characterize a liberal democracy (138, pp. 28–55) and they
insist that only Nazi ideals must be hammered into the children. Schooling in both countries employs strict disciplinary
methods within the classroom by placing more stress on
physical rather than mental training; and extra-curricular
activities are regulated in semi- or direct military fashion
(175, pp. 68–73). Thus inside the school children are taught
the theories of their régimes and outside they are made to
feel that even while immature they are able to put these
ideals into practice (140). The special, thorough schools for
prospective leaders in Germany resemble Plato's proposal in
his *Republic*. The culmination of German education is a half
or a full year of compulsory "labor service" (where classes
on Nazi doctrines are also held) and two years of military
service (20, pp. 174–182). In Nazi universities, among whose
entrance requirements both labor and military service are included, the social sciences and most of the humanities have
been destroyed, because German ways must be felt, not analyzed away (59).

The Russian régime also requires that its children grow
into good communists, but its periodicals (17) reveal con-
troversies concerning the best methods of indoctrination. The
American progressive movement, especially the teachings of
John Dewey, has been influential in Russia, and one reads
continually the plea that coöperation should be secured vol-
untarily and not imposed from above. Children must agree
with the official outlook, but they must be brought to agree
through dialectical means; *viz.*, through group discussion

with the teacher and through participation in the life of the country the synthetic outlook should be made to emerge. The basic Marxian contention concerning human nature that it is a product of the economic relations pervading a society finds its concrete embodiment in the field of social psychiatry where officials attempt to prevent frustrations by removing potentially frustrating conditions in the environment (186).

Thus democratic, fascist, and communist children are frustrated, as they are educated to become, respectively, good democrats, fascists, and communists. American students, in spite of the fact that few of them actually receive direct vocational guidance (11, p. 72), tend to emerge from school with the hope that the frustrations of education have prepared them for a job; Italians, Germans, and Russians are supposed to feel themselves a part of their state. Americans believe the gratifications they have a right to obtain will be personal; Germans and Italians say their duty is to support the state regardless of the fate of their own gratifications; and the Russians hope that by upholding the faith they will be gratified and their state will also be strengthened. To estimate the amount of frustration under the three systems is impossible; certainly schooling is more uniform and makes more demands in fascist and communist countries, but uniformity and compulsions are not necessarily correlated with increased frustration.

RESOCIALIZATION OF ADULTS

ALL four nations continually change and require, consequently, changed citizens. To be compelled to adjust to new conditions is frustrating, since older goal-responses encounter new interferences. A concept like Ogburn's "social lag" (124, pp. 199–265), for example, is a sociological way of implying some of the frustrations caused by a changing society and the resocialization such a society requires.

In America changes are brought about by new inventions

(like the cotton picker or any more efficient piece of machinery) and by new social schemes (like the New Deal or a
third political party). Those who support the older ways,
the field or factory worker and the individualistically minded
entrepreneur, are frustrated, and either become aggressive
toward the innovation, develop substitute responses, do both,
or become demoralized. Formally, however, the American
democracy imposes no rigid patterns upon these frustrated
people. Some of them are more or less free to protest, but
whether or not they conform to the requirements of the
changed conditions depends upon them. The numerous so-
called "social problems" which persist in America indicate
that people are allowed to remain frustrated and aggressive.
Solutions in a democracy simply do not emerge in accordance with a fixed, rigid plan; even formal laws frequently lag
behind conditions that have already changed.

At the same time Americans occasionally isolate a group
to repress and reform: the cries that are raised against
"reds," "atheists," and "un-Americans" testify to this. Such
groups, up to the present time, have had no great degree of
permanence. Their persecutors are more interested in expressing their own aggression than in resocializing them.

Under a dictatorship—whether of the fascist or communist type—it is the older people who are especially frustrated
as a result of the change of régime, for they have been socialized under previous standards. Democrats, liberals, pro-
gressives, all dissenters are wiped out by fascists—and wip-
ing out means torture, concentration camp, or outward conformity. Mothers are almost powerless to protest when they
find their family life tends to be destroyed as their children
dash off to participate in some activity demanded by the *Hitler Jugend* or the *Avanguardisti*. Hitler's attempts to change
religious practices have certainly frustrated some Catholics
and Protestants. Stalin—and before him Lenin stated the
theory and started the practice—is liquidating the enemies

of the revolution deliberately; the new technique in this connection has been, of course, the mass trial.

Under a dictatorship, moreover, the groups being resocialized are those which can be identified on the basis of some criterion: in Germany it is the Jews and "Bolsheviks"; in Italy it is the "Communists" and more recently the Jews; in Russia it is the "counter-revolutionaries," the "Trotskyites," and the "bourgeoisie." The enemies of the state are not individuals, they are distinguishable groups of individuals. Their change or their cultural annihilation, though apparently arbitrary to the victims themselves and to outsiders, always follows a general plan which is part of the state's total philosophy. And, finally, all enthusiastic adults are kept outwardly enthusiastic through propaganda; such "cultural renewing" (the Nazi phrase), requiring as it does novel ways of living, is inevitably frustrating.

In resocializing some of its inhabitants Russia, however, has often adopted a policy of gradualism. Lenin's reversion to an earlier capitalist form in his New Economic Policy is a vivid illustration of socialist compromise. The relative independence accorded the eleven republics within the nation and the continual stress that their cultures must not be regimented into one culture is another way of diminishing the frustration of change (178, V. 2, pp. 893–897); in this connection even the name "Russia" has been eliminated from the official title of the country. The Communist party, moreover, endeavors to eliminate racial prejudices and religious attitudes.

In regard to the problem of resocializing adults who do not conform, there is a basic difference between a democracy and a dictatorship. The latter develops an out-group within the in-group and plans to rid itself of that group through expulsion or assimilation. Americans, however, very rarely form such a group—usually individuals and not identifiable groups of people must socialize themselves gradually, or at least try to do so.

ECONOMIC AND SOCIAL FRUSTRATIONS

NEITHER under democracy, fascism, nor communism does fruit tumble into people's laps, nor is every man a hero. Basic and more culturally derived instigations cannot be satisfied automatically. Everywhere there is scarcity, natural or artificially created; everywhere there are regulations which destroy freedom of expression in any absolute sense.

Even the most bigoted believer in democracy is forced to recognize the existence of poverty. Through economic competition with their fellows some Americans always are unable to obtain the positions they most desire (11, p. 132); and millions are unemployed in a society which by placing a premium upon employment fails adequately to teach the individual suitable recreational habits. Those who are employed, whether they like their kind of work on the whole or not, are compelled to be punctual, to accept wages they consider too low (11, pp. 125–126, 210), to tolerate people (like foremen or bosses) whom they detest, and to repress their individualistic tendencies toward variation (11, p. 38). More and more workers, furthermore, have begun to believe that they will not be able to rise higher than their present job, that the American tradition of mobility is dying or dead (11, pp. 128–130; 95, p. 72). This is industry in a highly rationalized stage, a culture complex that pervades almost the entire world, especially occidental countries.

Fascism and communism, however, have invented new twists to this industrial pattern, some of which probably create additional frustrations. In a fascist society the stated goal of the industrial process is production and not consumption, in order to achieve economic autarchy. Italians and Germans are made to think of themselves as producers for the state and not as consumers who eventually enjoy their products (80; 123; 175, p. 99). Workers are enrolled in the "syndicates" in Italy and in the "Labor Front" in Germany; in practically every instance they must obey their employer who in turn usually has to obey the leaders of the country (20, pp. 141–142; 42, p. 133). No form of the strike is tolerated. In Germany, moreover, the peasant is tied to his plot of land through a complicated set of decrees (20, pp. 231–268). The fascist, therefore, toils, he is asked to believe, not for himself but for his fatherland. The strong body of secret police enforces the dictates of the national plan. It is very likely, especially since wages under fascism have decreased (175, pp. 35–37), that these hardships which have to be endured are frustrating, although it will be pointed out below that such belittling of the self in favor of the state may also furnish gratification.

In Russia one also finds an emphasis upon production, but at the same time the consumer has his separate organizations (178, V. 1, Chap. IV). In theory the masses control the political, social, and economic life of the country; but it seems to be true that during the present "transition stage" the real leaders of the country who are at the top of Russia's pyramidal system of government do not necessarily follow the dictates of the groups underneath, a circumstance that may be quite frustrating to the latter who have to obey. The Communist party has always had great difficulty in "collectivizing" the peasants (178, V. 1, pp. 233–284), and the suspicion may be adduced that peasants must be frustrated for the sake of conformity. It is not possible to follow the exact trend of wages, but apparently working hours have been decreased and vacation privileges are now more numerous (175, p. 36).

A democracy is also composed of large numbers of social groups which compete with one another for prestige and new members. The plight of the *nouveau riche* is notorious and an indication that the path to the status of being socially élite is strewn with frustrations. The bickerings and quarrels characteristic of some families and many friendships tend to frustrate the participants. The cruel rumors which pursue those who violate American mores are never amusing to the individuals concerned.

These practices also pervade fascist and communist societies. Their content and direction may be different, but their social rôle and the frustrations they cause may be almost identical. The existence of an enormous bureaucracy concerned with administration and discipline under a dictatorship must be frustrating to workers and others who can perceive that these bureaucrats, especially in the fascist countries, receive the preferred, more lucrative positions.

RACE PREJUDICE

Up to this point the characteristic frustrations of democracy, fascism, and communism have been indicated. The next step in the application of the frustration-aggression hypothesis is to plot the course of the ensuing aggression in accordance with the regulations of each of the societies. Before this is done, however, it is necessary to consider the problem of race prejudice. For, according to the hypothesis, the existence of a social prejudice against a group of people is evidence, first, that those who have the prejudice have been frustrated and, secondly, that they are expressing their aggression or part of it in fairly uniform fashion. Race prejudice, then, can be explained with the help of the present hypothesis and simultaneously as a problem it serves as a concrete illustration of the relationship between frustration and aggression.

In the United States the most patent race prejudice is toward the Negroes; some of the groups which have more recently migrated to America (like the Irish or the Japanese) are also treated with discrimination. In Italy the Northern Italian frowns upon his Southern countrymen and of late upon the Jews. Russia, as has been said, is attempting to eliminate most forms of race prejudice. It is the German persecution of the Jews with which American readers are most concerned and therefore this prejudice will be treated in some detail. The Negro situation in America has already been described elsewhere by Dollard (35) in terms of the hypothesis.

Race prejudice, according to the present view, is a form of aggression. Sometimes this aggression may be called *direct* when the frustrating object is identified. The race riots of post-war days in Chicago and East St. Louis are responses of this type: the invading and frustrating Negroes were known directly and resented. In other situations the aggression must be called *displaced* when the group toward whom the aggression is directed is not the frustrating one. Here the aggression is shifted from within the in-group on to people belonging to an out-group. Frequently, for example, individuals are known to be prejudiced who have had no direct contact with the objects of prejudice (82, p. 99).

Since most aggressive responses, including those involving race prejudice, are usually taboo for all members of a society, specific social permission must be given to those who wish to be aggressive toward a racial group. Two forms of such permission are recognized. The first is *rivalry*. In California local farmers are allowed to be aggressive toward the Japanese, for it is alleged that the latter, with their lower standards of living, constitute a real competitive threat to the former. *Traditional patterning* identifies another group of circumstances in which the aggression may be expressed. Here direct rivalry need not be present as a matter of fact; the existence of a pattern identifying a scapegoat group is sufficient. It may be true that, wherever such social "permission to hate" persists, its origin in the first place may be traced to actual competition.

For race prejudice to occur, not only must there be frustration and ensuing aggression, not only must there be permission to be aggressive but there must also be a way of identifying the people to be hated. Such identification is necessary in order to avoid the mistake of being aggressive toward an in-group member and it may assume various forms: racial stigmata (Negroes), national differences (French and Germans), language or religion (French Canadians), caste marks (India), social class (workers), and slave status. All of these differences have been employed by some one group which has attacked a subgroup.

In reference to Germany it is clear that post-war Germans were confronted with conditions which interfered with a variety of strongly instigated goal-responses. They were defeated in the war itself after an exhausting effort. They lost the "place in the sun" for which they had fought and their national prestige suffered a staggering blow. At Versailles and thereafter they had to admit defeat and the hopelessness of further aggression toward the conquerors; they were compelled to relinquish their colonies and additional territory, their navy was confiscated, their army was reduced to one adequate only for internal policing, and in almost every way they were made to feel a third-rate power. Nor can it be forgotten that millions of people were partially starved during the war and that large numbers of Germans had to abandon military careers. Economically, too, the country remained frustrated. The inflation of German currency brought loss and misery to the middle class and interfered with the plans of all others who were attempting to achieve personal security through saving. Less than a decade later the world-wide depression reached a German people who had never experienced even a temporary prosperity since the last gun had been fired.

If it be presumed that almost every German experienced and resented at least some of these various frustrations personally, it is clear that aggression would increase and would be expressed in one form or another. Direct aggression toward the Allies was not possible; such a response had already failed and had been punished in part by new frustrations. At the close of the war the old monarchy had been replaced by the Weimar democracy through a revolution, certainly a directly and overtly aggressive act. But frustration remained and increased the strength of instigation to aggression. As Germans began to appreciate their humiliating position in the eyes of the world and as the economic life of the country declined, this aggression had to be displaced. Its displacement assumed diverse forms. First there was the rapid growth in membership of the Social Democratic party and especially of the Communist party, both of which gave their supporters an opportunity to voice their hatreds against the existing social order. The in-group was further disrupted by intense rivalries among the numerous political parties—at the time Hitler assumed control there were twenty-seven of them. The youth movement, modernism, and other attacks on the old moral standards must also be interpreted as displaced aggression.

The middle and upper classes of German society soon realized that this display of aggression against the state and the social order would threaten their own positions. For this reason many of them were willing to support the National Socialist German Workers party, as Hitler called his movement. This party sought to be overtly aggressive toward the republic which had not prevented what was considered antisocial aggression; toward Russia which symbolized the rise of a proletarian state internationally; toward the Treaty of Versailles and the European order it had established; and toward an internal scapegoat group, the Jews. After gaining power as a result of skillful propaganda that embodied these aggressive demands, the support of important members of the upper class, and shrewd political strategy, only two acts of aggression in the Nazi program could be executed immediately. The Republic and its supporters were destroyed and an organized pogrom descended upon the Jews.

Jews were ideal victims for the aggression of the German people. Some of them had profited from the inflation, as had Gentiles; and some of them occupied important positions in the professions, in government, and in business, as did Gentiles. It was easy, consequently, for Nazi propagandists to suggest that Jews and Jews alone were economic rivals. The presence of a number of foreign Jews, especially from Poland, and of other Jews who had not been completely acculturated was used as evidence of a cultural threat. Anti-Semitism, moreover, had always existed in Germany and it was possible to resurrect and to strengthen this traditional patterning. In these ways aggression toward Jews was rationalized, and by means of official edicts social permission was given to engage in direct as well as in subtle and indirect attacks upon them.

Nor was it any more difficult to identify Jews as the outgroup which should be hated. The basis for the differentiation started from the Jewish religion and was extended to embrace allegedly racial behavior. The really foreign Jews in Germany were used as evidence that all Jews were essentially "different" from Germans, and through exaggerating propaganda it was possible to ascribe to every Jew the Yiddish language and the orthodoxy in clothes and bearing that characterized only a few of them.

German persecution of the Jews, in short, is aggression that has been displaced from the agents really responsible for the frustration. This aggression is now only one segment of the pattern of modern Germany. Gradually through a bold foreign policy, through rearmament, and through the conciliatory attitude of the English upper classes which has diminished the anticipation of punishment, Hitler has managed to be aggressive toward the very countries which were victorious in 1918. The more recent attacks on Jews suggest, in addition to the obvious economic advantages involved, that such displacement is still necessary.

THE DIRECTION OF AGGRESSION

According to the concepts that have been employed, much of the aggression which results from the frustration imposed by these three political systems is displaced to substitute objects. The question concerning the "true" cause of the frustration is of great academic significance, but it cannot be answered glibly even by theoreticians. Nor can it be answered in any absolute sense by Americans, Italians, Germans, or Russians themselves. Yet every individual perceives what he imagines to be "the cause" of his thwartings. Since it is assumed that the strongest instigation is to acts of aggression directed against the agent perceived to be the source of the frustration, such perceptions, whether correct or not, will play an important rôle in determining the direction of aggression.

Americans advertise themselves as "masters of their fate." Concretely this means that Americans tend to blame only themselves for their frustrations and that they incline to be self-aggressive when they fail. To place responsibility in this fashion is the essence of what is sometimes called "the pioneer tradition" in American life. It is part of the individualism of the business man to proclaim not only that he does not require aid from the government, but that such aid, if and when it is forced upon him, will hinder his own efforts to be successful (95, p. 449). Men who fail, therefore, frequently turn the aggression they experience upon themselves and mumble that "things would have been different if *I* had been able to . . ." The dominant Protestant religion, as Max Weber has shown in somewhat exaggerated fashion (179), helps to foster this general feeling that it is the duty of the individual to seek virtue, to avoid evil, and to be held culpable if he deviates from the path of righteousness.

The task of the Communist organizer in America has been made difficult by the presence of this trait within potential converts. Why should an American abuse the boss or the system when the fault, he believes, has been his own (95, p. 41)? Since the depression and the recession have led to governmental agencies which directly affect the lives of individual citizens, however, there has been a growing tendency for American workers to direct aggression from themselves on to their employers (11, p. 213; 95, pp. 450–451). Even college students have been instructed systematically through courses in the social sciences that "society" is really responsible for many of the problems confronting individuals. The guess may be hazarded, nevertheless, that great sections of the middle class still believe that they themselves cause their own frustration or success, still think that it is they alone who can and must bring the prosperity now hiding beyond a corner, and still take it for granted that the ideology of the pioneer era is applicable to the interdependent society in which we now live.

People living under dictatorships may also hold themselves responsible for their individual failures, but officially they are given a blanket explanation which may actually enable them to blame members of an out-group and hence be aggressive toward them. In Germany frustrations are said to be due to the machinations of that country's enemies. The frustrations of the past are traced to Jews, to bankers, to Marxists. The frustrations of the present which the four-year plan requires are necessary because of these same enemies and especially because of the hostile democratic and communistic countries outside of Germany's borders (13). Thus race prejudice allows Germans to be aggressive toward a scapegoat group not only for past but also for many present and future frustrations. Germans must endure *Ersatz* products since France and England have not yet entered into another Munich agreement to return the former African colonies. People must relinquish fats and desserts in order to help arm the fatherland which still faces a hostile world. The situation in Italy is somewhat similar (175, p. 53) ; until at least recently not so much aggression has been displaced upon the Jews.

Russia displaces aggression, perhaps to a lesser degree, by telling her people why they have been miserable and why the maximum of gratification is not yet theirs. Here the following assertions are made. The old exploiters, the clique which gathered around the Czars, it is said, deprived the nation of its just benefits and even kept the population illiterate. When the Communist party threw out the Mensheviks, it had to begin construction upon this shaky foundation. Throughout its five-year plans it has been hindered continually by wreckers from within (the enemies of the state described above) and by belligerent capitalist and now fascist nations from without. The population is informed, therefore, that it must make sacrifices in the meantime if plenty in the future is to be secured; and the failure of a detail of a plan is blamed not on the plan, not on a member of the régime itself, but on an individual belonging to one of the hostile groups which usually in turn is said to be supported by one of the nations opposed to Russia.

In all three societies, then, certain patterns exist which tend to determine who shall be perceived as the source of frustrations and hence to influence the direction of aggression. In the fascist countries these patterns of perception coincide with patterns of permission. Not all of the aggression, however, can be disposed of in the approved ways and therefore each culture attempts to regulate the expression of the vast amount of aggression that remains. It is necessary, therefore, to describe the various channels through which this aggression is or is not released in democracy, fascism, and communism.

American school children, as has been explained above, are required to develop coöperative habits in the classroom; i.e., they are seldom allowed to be overtly aggressive. It is a blow to their teachers to witness the ease with which they throw aside these coöperative habits almost as soon as school is dismissed. Then direct competition in sports or indirect identification with aggressive heroes like athletes, Indians, or G-men is clearly discernible. Aggression against parents, though not tolerated, nevertheless exists, especially during the period of adolescence. But on the whole the American adolescent begins to assume the responsibilities of citizenship after he has been convinced that the accepted way in which he may release his energies, whether aggressively, constructively, or both, is by seeking economic and social advancement.

In trying to improve his economic status the individual in a democracy is theoretically free to compete rather ruthlessly with his fellows. When he works more vigorously, when he arranges clever business "deals," or when he succeeds in outwitting his competitor in almost any form, he advances himself and secures prestige in the eyes of most of his friends. These activities result not only from instigation to self-betterment but also, as was emphasized in Chapter IV, from frustrations during childhood and from others imposed by different social institutions during adulthood; they can be considered, therefore, at least partially a form of displaced aggression. At the same time, in being aggressive the competing individual dare not transgress certain laws or mores, for then he will be punished either formally or informally. The Supreme Court is stern when it regulates competition in terms of the Bill of Rights or especially through what is called so euphemistically "due process of law"; criminal action is brought against individuals who better their status or express aggression by becoming delinquents or criminals; a man is accused of disobeying the dictum of "fair play" when he deviates from the cultural norm either on the athletic field or in business. Some of these taboos in a democracy are clearly formulated, others are rather vague and elastic in their application.

Not everyone, to be sure, is successful or prosperous. The frustrated worker, doomed to monotony and insecurity, tends to grow more sympathetic toward unions, not only in order to raise his wages and shorten his hours of work, but also as a means of expressing aggression against the employer. He seldom murders or strikes the man who discharges him or cuts his weekly income; he growls, departs, and then blames himself or perhaps joins a union (11, pp. 213–215). The movements of irrational intolerance toward minorities which sweep the country, especially during a depression, are symptomatic of the strong instigation to aggression that men possess and undoubtedly, by the principle of catharsis, serve to deflect aggression from the frustrator to a scapegoat (95, p. 443). The popularity of the athletic contest, the motion picture, and the pulp press must also indicate the same tendency to flee from frustrations by seeking an approved channel through which aggression may be expressed and substitute responses developed (11, Chap. V; 13, Chap. VII). The sweeping victory of Franklin Roosevelt in 1932 can be accounted for at least partially when it is remembered that this election occurred in the midst of a depression, that millions of Americans were badly frustrated, and that they therefore sought to be aggressive against the Hoover régime in this sanctioned political way. The somewhat dismal memory which many Americans have of their own school days (even though they frequently disguise their feelings by extolling their "happy childhood") and their jibes at the impracticality of part of their education are verbal reflections of the aggression that has been generated by the frustrations imposed

upon them by their former teachers and by the disillusion-
ment caused by the discrepancy between the ideals they were
taught and the practices they are forced to encounter.

America, therefore, contains diffuse aggression, a part of
which certain groups attempt to guide away from themselves.
Many of the vehicles of communication still extol "the American Dream," i.e., the opportunity open to everyone to rise
from a lower to a higher economic plane; thus the process of
displacing aggression from possible frustrating agents on to
the frustrated themselves serves the function of preventing
social outbreaks. More directly, the employing class continually stresses its own benevolence (as illustrated by the Community Chest and other forms of private charity and by an
enlightened industrial philosophy) and directly or subtly
asks its workers to place their faith not in union organizers
or agitators but in that class. Americans usually are neither
fanatically devoted nor opposed to their leaders, since they
tend not to assign to the latter responsibility for their suc-
cesses and failures.

In the social life of the United States caste barriers are
resented keenly, for example, by certain racial groups. Those
who feel the discrimination, even though they cannot kick
these barriers aside, are able, nevertheless, to seek both retaliation and opportunities for substitute behavior by forming their own cliques or organizations, most of which tend to
assume the pattern of the groups from which the frustrated
are excluded. Sociologically this procedure can be called a
simple case of diffusion; but psychologically it is clear, or
should be clear, that aggression and substitute response are
the mechanisms that cause the culture traits to descend.

From this survey of the direction of aggression in America, certain conclusions follow. In the first place, even though
the theory of a democracy states that frustrations are the
responsibility of the individual and that whatever aggression
results should be self-aggression, Americans in practice give

overt expression to their aggression in diverse ways. Then it is clear that sociologically much of this aggression is turned against certain of the in-groups which exist in America and against other in-groups which are deliberately formed sporadically. Aggression, however, has been seldom directed against one single out-group and hence in-group cohesion tends to be weak, except during a war or temporarily during a national campaign like the N.R.A. at its inception. As a result, individual, social, and industrial conflicts have characterized the American democracy; at the moment, however, there appears to be a strong tendency for Americans to feel more unified as a result of fascist activities here and in South America.

In contrast fascist and communist countries present an external appearance of internal calm, an illusion every naïve tourist loves to report. Under a fascist rule, as has been suggested above, people from infancy onward are told that they must be frustrated because of the wicked groups that are threatening the fatherland both internally and externally. Theirs is not a land in which the blessings of gratification can be expected to be distributed automatically to every inhabitant; rather theirs is the fate to be frustrated for the benefit of the state. Everywhere in Germany, even on coins, *Gemeinnutz vor Eigennutz* shrieks at people; in Italy, people make sacrifices in the name of *Risorgimento*. The bitter hymns of hate against Jews and foreign nations that are unleashed by the German press and radio have served to direct smouldering aggressions away from momentary, frustrating circumstances and have enabled Germans—and more recently Austrians and Sudetens too—to persecute innocent men and women sadistically and to await the next "day" when ruthless war can be waged.

It cannot be forgotten that a fascist country is efficiently policed and that, therefore, the spontaneous release of aggression in any overt form against the established order is

almost completely prohibited by anticipation of severe punishment. It would be interesting in this connection to be able
to quote comparative crime figures over a period of time, but
such figures are either unavailable or else the task of interpretation is impossible. For a crime rate, as has been shown
in Chapter VI, is not only symptomatic of latent aggression
and of the punishments people anticipate as a result of the
mechanisms of social control, but it is also a function of the
definition given to an anti-social act. In Italy crimes against
the state can be said to have fluctuated when one attempts to
reduce the available figures to identical periods of time (a
most risky procedure) ; homicides and criminal assaults have
also fluctuated (175, pp. 116–117). During the first and
second years of Hitler's régime in Germany, petty and major
thefts and homicides decreased, whereas murders increased
(175, pp. 116–117). These figures, regardless of the trends
they suggest, are remarkable, for they show that some crimes
do persist in Italy and Germany, i.e., that some people are
still able to be overtly aggressive. And it is significant that
"the number of suicides in Italy has increased from year to
year" (175, p. 116), since suicide is the supreme act of aggression turned against the self.

It is evident, however, that under fascism the potential
leaders of the frustrated have to mutter silently in their un-
derground quarters. Strict censorship of all the media of
communication effectively prevents the verbal expression of
aggression. Instead there are jokes, the point of which may
be a sly attack upon the national heroes. Those who con-
sciously oppose the régime derive almost pathological glee
from small, petty infractions of official regulations. Abuse is
heaped upon traitors of the ruling clique who recently have
been exposed; thus the tales told in Germany concerning
Ernst Röhm must be traced, it can be supposed, to the fact
that this slain trooper once used to employ the familiar form
in addressing Hitler, the one individual toward whom no ag-

gression is permitted. Displacing aggression from Hitler, the supreme source of gratifications and punishments, to his less loved and less formidable advisers is evidently a device that is used very frequently by Germans who are dissatisfied with the progress of the régime, if informal conversation be acceptable as evidence. Such displacement, moreover, may also suggest one of the functions of the mass trials in Russia: to leave Stalin's reputation stainless by placing responsibility for frustration upon other high officials. It may also account for the fact that Franklin Roosevelt is much more popular than his close associates; a *Fortune* Quarterly Survey (44), for example, has reported that 54.8 per cent of Americans "approve in general of" the President and 80.3 per cent "like his personality," whereas only 28.3 per cent "like his advisers and associates."

Fascism has other ways of reducing instigation to aggression. The youth who have been disciplined so severely in the German schools are compelled to drain swamps or build barracks before they can enter industry or the university; the catharsis thus involved may be considerable. The war games and even the mass athletic pageants also allow Germans and Italians to express themselves, if only in a substitute way. That many of the inhabitants in these fascist countries can hatch their plots only in dreams, both literally and figuratively, is a fact to be inferred from the status of the worker who dares not protest directly when he feels that he has been treated unjustly; or it is a fact which only the reports of refugees can substantiate selectively.

The frustrations of fascism, like those of democracy, are numerous, but the ensuing aggressions are released in a rather uniform fashion which coincides, more or less, with the direction which the régime prescribes. For the overt expressions of aggression are approved only when they are directed toward the official enemies and when they are part of the sanctioned program. At the moment there dare not be departures, and so whatever superfluous aggression remains must become non-overt.

Since the entire structure of contemporary Russia is built, theoretically at least, upon the principle of a pyramid, there is some expectation that the individual is able to express a portion of the aggression he possesses through this system of government. Even now a certain amount of discussion and freedom is encouraged before a policy is adopted officially (178, V. 1, pp. 22-28, 36-40); thereafter no dissent is tolerated and opposition must be repressed either permanently or until a new policy is proposed. Obviously such a procedure enables every Russian to express some of his aggression, especially in his local factory or village group. But, inasmuch as the decisions of the population do not determine at all completely the policies of Stalin, a local election may afford momentary catharsis without having the intended social consequences.

Every Russian is encouraged to improve the economic state of the country as aggressively as possible, provided that he works within the national plan and causes no waste of human or natural resources. "Socialistic competition" between the "shock-brigades" of rival factories in order to increase efficiency and productivity, the "Stakhanovite" system to boost the output of the individual worker, and the denunciation through loss of prestige and ridicule of laggards indicate how the Communists regulate the aggression within their people (178, V. 2, Chap. IX). Russian peasants are usually guarded so that they will not sabotage any aspect of the agrarian economy (178, V. 1, pp. 250-284).

Like the fascist school system, education in Russia provides its students with a rather closely knit view of the world and of the destiny of Communism. Marxism and Leninism guide the curriculum and, together with a police force, serve to impress Russian youth with the nature of their obligations and of the aggressions that are strongly taboo. The mass trials emphasize the identity of the state's enemies and warn prospective "saboteurs" of the punishment they may anticipate if they do not conform. The alleged fact that "the majority of crime in the Soviets is of a picayune nature (in their opinion)" (175, p. 116) can be interpreted as showing either a significant diminution of frustration or the effects of the advanced system of penology or both. It must be said of Russians, as it has been said of Germans and Italians, that they too are allowed to direct their overt aggression only in the prescribed way. "The rest is silence"—or non-overt aggression.

GRATIFICATIONS

In describing the frustrations and aggressive behavior generated by democracy, fascism, and communism, it is also necessary to outline what seem to be the major gratifications offered by the three political systems. For, since there is no exact way of measuring the amount of frustration and aggression, a knowledge of gratification helps to suggest some of the situations in which aggression does not appear because substitute responses are possible. Analyzing a society merely in terms of frustration and aggression is too one-sided; adding gratification may tend to make the total picture clearer. When frustrations are contrasted with gratifications, moreover, it is tempting and important to try to compare democracy, fascism, and communism in these respects; unfortunately no clear-cut comparison is possible with the inadequate data that are available. The method of comparison that might be employed in demonstrating the different ways gratification is patterned may be stated, however, even though no definitely quantitative conclusions can be drawn.

The subject of sexual gratification is important, but it is one on which there is no satisfactory information and concerning which psychological interpretation is not possible. Dictators in both Germany and Italy encourage childbearing, although Mussolini's policy has not raised the birthrate. The United States probably places the greatest stigma upon illegitimacy, Russia the least, and Germany and Italy rank closer to Russia than to America. Mothers and infants are protected by all four countries. Contraceptives under most circumstances are prohibited in Italy, they are being outlawed in Germany, they are permitted but not always available in Russia, and their status in America is varying. Divorces are easiest to obtain in Russia and in some states of the United States; they are permitted in Germany, and they are practically non-existent in Italy. From a *legal* point of view, then, Russia offers the greatest amount of sexual freedom and Italy the least (175, Chap. XIV), but there is no point-for-point relationship between legal permission and actual gratification.

Nor is it any easier to analyze democracy, fascism, and communism in terms of economic standards, i.e., gratifications in respect to more basic impulses. Whether or not a so-called higher standard of living leads to the gratification or the frustration of the additional instigated goal-responses to which it gives rise in an issue that must be raised but that cannot be answered satisfactorily. It seems certain, however, that in terms of gross consumption the United States has the highest standard of living; and that this country and Russia are more affluent than Germany (including her recent acquisitions of Austria and parts of Czechoslovakia) and Italy in respect to mineral resources, forests, and (to a varying degree) agricultural products (175, pp. 13–14, 22–28). And yet the contrasts between the rich and the poor in America are staggering and the billions of dollars which must be spent for relief and on government projects leave no doubt that millions of Americans are far from being gratified in any fundamental sense.

The huge expenditures (in proportion to total population and governmental receipts) to equip and maintain the military machine in Italy, Germany, and Russia (175, pp. 97, 104) require extremely high tax rates or other sacrifices and therefore decrease the possibility of securing maximum gratification in those countries. Italy's standard of living has never been very high, but there are some shaky grounds for believing that it has been raised under Mussolini (175, pp. 49, 53), whereas Germany's has been higher than it is at the present time (175, pp. 49–55); and so *perhaps* (and the word "perhaps" must be placed in italics, since here too only speculation is possible) Germans feel more frustrated than Italians, since their culture has given them previously a greater number of impulses which now are frustrated. Before the October revolution the Russians also existed on a low standard of living; this standard has been raised by the communist régime, although it does not yet even approach American standards and although prices on Soviet standards are still very high (175, pp. 49–55); it may be guessed that this relative rise has been gratifying to some of the inhabitants of that country.

In America the major gratifications seem to be experienced in terms of the individual's own existence. Has he been successful, has he had a happy marriage, will his children be more secure than he has been, is he respected by his fellows, has he seen the latest movie? These are the questions which Americans ask themselves to a lesser or greater degree and, when the answers are affirmative, people feel gratified. Workers and farmers, to be sure, dare ask themselves only a few, but all of them doubtless aspire to be able to concern themselves with such activities if and when they ever can be more secure. The American locus of gratification, consequently, is in the person and in his home. There are indications, nevertheless, that the American sometimes tends to believe that his own gratifications are linked to the gratification of a larger group than his immediate family. Identifications with the neighborhood, the community, the fraternal or professional organization exist and are indeed quite powerful. Nor can it be denied that Americans are patriotic and that they are proud of their traditions and contemporary exploits. But such ties are not considered absolutely essential to gratification, even though their significance is not overlooked. The feeling of mutual interdependence, except during a war, is not so strong as the liberal theorists of the eighteenth and nineteenth centuries believed that it was. Theoretically the man on the production line may be a necessary link in the chain of economic and social activity which enables the democratic system to survive, but more often than not he must think of his weekly wage and not of the relationship between his job and the rest of the country.

Under a fascist or a communist dictatorship the situation seems to be quite different; or at least the official propaganda tries to make people feel differently. It has been pointed out that in Italy a job is not merely a way of earning money with which to purchase the necessities of living; it is an integral part of Mussolini's scheme to expand the Italian Empire and to fortify the fascist place in the universe. In Germany a job cannot, should not be considered in terms of its prosaic demands upon the individual; it is a significant way of contributing one's share to the Leader whose only care is the welfare and the protection of the fatherland. In Russia, a job is much more than its motions; it is another step in the direction of communism through the assistance it gives the national plan. The gratifications offered by working in a fascist or a communist country thus are somewhat religious in nature, when by religion is understood the belief that overt gratification is not obtainable at the moment but is deferred ultimately for the future. The Christian expects to find this ultimate gratification in the hereafter, the fascist in the growth of a powerful state, and the communist in the communism designed for his descendants. In the meantime, as a result of such phantasies, the expenditure of energy in Germany, Italy, and Russia *may* be more gratifying and more meaningful than in America. Dictators, moreover, offer more than hopes; each one can refer to concrete accomplishments like paved roads, houses for workers, leisure organizations, social schemes, and the curbing of old abuses, all of which are dramatized by a minister of propaganda (175, *passim;* 178, V. 2, Chaps. X, XI).

Incorporating the individual into a huge plan which transcends him, if this incorporation actually does take place, is a phenomenon that cannot be overlooked when an understanding of and prediction concerning modern fascism and communism are desired. To reason from economic statistics that one country is more or less frustrated than another may be correct, but only in respect to the particular frustration which conceivably may result from the conditions giving rise to those statistics. Since all frustrations occur within individuals, no one frustration can be singled out nor from it can one deduce that aggressive behavior inevitably will increase or decrease. Italians may have less Chianti, but the Italian flag now floats over most of Ethiopia. Germans may have to deprive themselves of meat and fruits, but Vienna and Sudetenland are now part of the Reich. Russians occasionally still have to stand in queues even for basic commodities, but their country now manufactures articles that formerly had to be imported. Let no man say, with our present information, that a pudding is necessarily more or less gratifying than a pageant. Dictators try to replace puddings with pageants and with strong identification between many of their countrymen and themselves. People cannot subsist completely on abstractions and symbols, and so there must be a limit (as yet undefined in a rigorous sense) to which some gratifications can serve as substitutes for others.

A final word must be added concerning a time factor. Clinical evidence seems to indicate that some aggression can remain in a non-overt form for long periods of time without

any appreciable overt expression, or without the development of severe neuroses, but it is not at all clear how long
large groups of people in a society can do likewise. And so it
must be said that, *if* people under dictatorships (and in a
democracy for that matter) are so severely frustrated as the
evidence might indicate, *if* the gratifications are not sufficiently compensating, and *if* they are not allowed to express
a great deal of their aggression overtly, they eventually will
seek overt forms for themselves. During the post-revolution-
ary days, while fascism and communism were new, the old
guard and many others derived gratification from seeing
their ideals realized or partially realized; but thereafter perhaps the frustrations have become more obnoxious. For this
reason the question must be asked whether communism can
achieve its goals rapidly enough to prevent massed uprisings; whether fascism inevitably and continually must offer
the release of war or whether drastic reforms or revolts will
come into existence; and whether, unless democracy too is
changed, it can survive.

CHAPTER VIII

A PRIMITIVE SOCIETY: THE ASHANTI

IT has been pointed out in Chapter IV that life in society is inevitably frustrating and that tendencies to aggressive behavior are continuously generated. Certain cultural adjustments, therefore, tend to be developed that prevent the destruction of the society. In this chapter an examination of the literature on the Ashanti[1] will be made in an effort to determine the extent to which there are these adjustments to frustration and aggression. From the theory of society already presented it is to be expected that aggressive acts which are socially undesirable will be strongly suppressed, whereas those that are not dangerous to social welfare will be permitted and those that serve socially useful ends will be demanded.

It is exceedingly difficult to make such an analysis with the type of anthropological data that lie at hand on most primitive societies. The literature on the Ashanti, though admirably complete, reveals certain unavoidable limitations from the point of view of the present research. Captain Rattray, the principal source of information, was not concerned with identifying aggressive behavior and frustrating conditions, and there are inevitable difficulties in interpreting his material. His description is couched predominantly in cultural terms. He reports, for the most part, patterned customs, partly inferred from direct observation and partly derived from answers given by the natives to his questions. The skeptical reader of ethnography often pulls himself up sharply with the question: Does the actual behavior of the natives

1. This society is a well-known West African tribe composed of people who are exceedingly powerful and warlike and whose fierceness in inter-tribal combat has struck terror along the Gold Coast and far into the interior.

really conform to such patterns? Frequently there is definite evidence to the contrary; thus, though adultery is stated to be prohibited and heavily penalized among the Ashanti, Rattray's actual observations show that cases of adultery are extremely common and are seldom brought into court. Recognition of the importance of historical influences, such as cultural diffusion, suggests, moreover, the advisability of accepting conclusions derived from the study of any single primitive society as in the highest degree tentative. Despite these difficulties, a study of the Ashanti may prove worthwhile if the frustration-aggression hypothesis leads to the discovery of relationships among phenomena that might otherwise seem discrete.[2]

CONTROL OF AGGRESSION

A SURVEY of Ashanti culture indicates that there are many restrictions placed upon expressions of aggression. Probably all acts which violate established prohibitions contain some admixture of aggression. That such acts are dangerous to society is clear in most cases. The sanction attached to transgression reflects the strength of the instigation to these acts as well as the importance of controlling them. If acts, therefore, which contain a high component of aggression are severely punished, the conclusion may be derived that they are powerfully instigated.

Treason against the state is regarded by the Ashanti as a purely aggressive act and is punished by death. Plotting to dethrone a chief or acting in any way to his detriment is a capital offense. To be captured by the enemy is to commit symbolic treason; hence a warrior is expected to commit suicide rather than submit to capture.

When the battle was going against them, an Ashanti Chief would

2. In another society, the Klamath Indians, Dr. Philleo Nash (121) has recognized a correlation between deprivation and religious revivalism as well as between deprivation and aggressive behavior against white settlers.

stand upon the Stool, an insult to his ancestral ghosts to fire their anger and make them fight more vigorously. As a last resort, Chief and war captains would blow themselves up along with the regalia, rather than fall into the hands of the enemy or violate the "oath" which they had taken before setting out on the campaign. There is a well-known Ashanti saying which runs . . . (If it is a choice between dishonour and death, death is preferable), and again . . . (If I go forward, I die; if I flee, I die; better to go forward and die in the mouth of battle). (131, p. 123)

The frustration-aggression hypothesis suggests that such acts as desertion normally contain an aggressive component which is directed against the king and his authority. This becomes clear if the culture pattern described above is made concrete by considering in detail the case of a warrior who surrenders to the enemy. It may be assumed that when this man leaves his home for the battlefield his strongest instigation is to go on living. He wants to be able to return to the enjoyment of those pleasures which characterize his daily life in Ashanti. In the midst of battle he is confronted with the grave possibility of being killed. This anticipation of interference with his desire to return to Ashanti is a frustration and the warrior is instigated to fight more vigorously against the enemies who threaten to take his life. If the odds now go strongly against him and fighting proves of no avail, his only escape from death may be to surrender to the enemy. In other words, the only way to keep on living may be to stop fighting and lay down his arms. But the oath which he took before battle and in which he promised his king to conquer or to die blocks this way of preserving his life. His desire to live is about to be thwarted by his promise. He knows, furthermore, that if he violates his oath and at any time returns home he will be put to death. He can no longer look forward to taking up life where he left off when he went into battle. These frustrations arouse aggression directed against the authority of the king. Fortified by this anger the warrior's determination to live, even though a captive, overrides social control and he surrenders to the foe. The Ashanti recognize this expression of revolt against authority as treason, and if the warrior is recaptured he will be given a trial and punished with death.

The natives regard murder as an aggressive act directed against the established authorities as well as against the victim:

> The set formula of denunciation by the judge at the trial of a murderer . . . seems to show that one reason for the abhorrence with which this offence was regarded arose from a determination to prevent the individual taking the law into his own hands. The power to "wield the knife," that is, to inflict capital punishment, always seems to have been one of the most jealously guarded prerogatives of the central authority. (131, p. 290)

The ghost of a murdered man, moreover, will haunt the people in their sleep and is especially likely to avenge himself upon any chief who allows the murder to pass unpunished. Consistent with the attitude that murder is an aggressive act directed against the central authority is the mos that killing in self-defense in no way mitigates the penalty.

In another place Rattray states:

> For a man to have killed the person who had offended him was to throw down a direct challenge to one who alone "held the knife," and was therefore an act which struck at the root of all centralized authority. This aspect seemed the one most emphasized at the trial which ensued, in which the murderer . . . was accused of not having brought his case before the Councillors that it might have been listened to with "good ears," but of having taken "a club to strike and kill the Akyeame," thus treating the council of Elders as if they were "brute beasts." The blow which struck down the dead man would thus appear to have been regarded as aimed also at the *maiestas* of the central authority. (131, p. 295)

An application of the frustration-aggression hypothesis

confirms the Ashanti interpretation that murder is an aggressive act directed in part against the state. This can be made explicit if the patterned procedure described above is considered as applying to a specific case. An analysis of the behavior of a man, for example, who commits murder in revenge for a deadly insult reveals the probable source of the aggression. Up to the time the insult is inflicted, this man may be assumed to be a respected member of the community. He hopes to keep on enjoying the admiration of his associates. But he then finds himself insulted. This is an affront that threatens to destroy his "good name." He is instigated to behave as a respected and admired member of the community, but these responses are frustrated by the offender and the man is moved to retaliate. Direct aggression against the person who insulted him, however, is prohibited by law. He cannot take the matter into his own hands and revenge himself upon the offender. He is supposed to bring the case before the court for trial. This is a further frustration. He is now angry not only with the man who insulted him but also with the authorities who interfere with his revenge tendencies. Armed with this anger he strikes the man who insulted him and kills him. By so doing he is venting aggression both against the offender and the state. It is this latter aspect of his instigation which is emphasized at the trial and for which he is sentenced to death.

A suggestion that the natives themselves connect aggression with frustration in the case of murder is found in a reply to an inquiry by Rattray concerning possible motives for murder. The informant said, in substance: "A man might have a great many debts, but instead of hanging himself, he might decide to kill some one else first, saying to himself, 'I shall then have a name, and also some one to go with me.' "

Even the killing of an enemy in wartime is rigidly controlled. Preferably the foe should first be captured and given an impromptu trial for treason on the battlefield, after which he may be executed without compunction. If the enemy is killed, however, the slayer must hold a similar trial over the body and then decapitate the corpse. To omit this formality is looked upon as an act of aggression against the state. The inference seems to be that indiscriminate killing, even in wartime, contains the germ of danger to the organized machinery of the society. Even in the heat of combat, therefore, a warrior is forced to remember that he is not killing wantonly but is the king's executioner carrying out the penalty for treason.

Suicide likewise is considered an affront to the established authorities, save under the most exceptional circumstances, and is regarded as a capital offense. Self-slaughter is an admission of guilt; it raises the presumption that the person has done something for which he deserves to be executed. By committing suicide, consequently, he is cheating justice and escaping the consequences of his crime. The Ashanti authorities meet such an emergency by giving the corpse a trial, cutting off its head, and barring its spirit from entering the land of the dead. The pronouncement made over the body reveals the nature of the instigation to this procedure:

[Addressing the Chief.] "This is your slave. No one knows what he had done, and today he has hanged himself." [Addressing the corpse.] "No man knows a single thing that came into your head, but because you did not bring your case here that we might take good ears to hear it, but took a club and struck the *Akyeame*—and when you kill us [thus] you regard us as brute beasts—therefore you are guilty!" (131, p. 300)

Actually this conception is not so alien to our own society, as is evidenced by the care which is taken to prevent the suicide of prisoners sentenced to death.

A pregnant woman is subject to a number of special taboos which are not immediately reasonable from our point of view. For example, she may not look upon a monkey or any deformity, and she must not allow little red ants to fall upon her. These and other restrictions may be interpreted, however, as prohibitions on expressing aggression toward the unborn child. Looking upon a monkey or a deformity is believed to have a harmful effect upon the foetus; if little red ants fall upon a pregnant woman she will be expected to have a miscarriage. The taboos become explicable when it is remembered that pregnancy ordinarily imposes a number of frustrations upon a woman. Her activities are interfered with during this time and she is haunted by the anticipation of a painful and dangerous delivery. Such frustrations as these arouse aggression against the foetus. A woman must not commit adultery during this period because this would kill her child. Those who come in contact with her must be extremely careful. For a person to say to her "You are pregnant" is a punishable offense; should a miscarriage follow, that person is held responsible and is heavily fined.

Certain other acts which symbolize intent to kill, and hence may be considered disguised or displaced forms of aggression, are regarded as seriously as if the deed were actually committed. These acts sometimes appear quite innocuous, such as proclaiming in public the intention not to eat again, allowing the head hair to grow long, and cutting something with a knife at right angles to the object.

Strangely enough, physical assault, though an aggressive act, is not regarded by the Ashanti as expressing intent to kill. To strike a person is interpreted primarily as an insulting act and is punished according to the prestige of the person assaulted. If the victim is a high official, the aggressor is executed because the blow insults the spirits of the departed kings and chiefs. Striking another person aggressively is one of the first acts prohibited in childhood. For a child to strike his parent is an extremely grave offense. It is interesting to note that both high officials and parents are surrogates of authority. They play the rôles of frustrating and socializing agents in the society. The spirits of departed kings and chiefs also symbolize authority. They are the supernatural agents of social control. According to the hypothesis these members of the society would be the most natural targets for aggression; and, as a matter of fact, it is just these individuals who are most strongly protected in this respect by taboos.

Verbal insults may be as severely punished as physical assault. A child is not permitted to speak abusively to his father; such an act invariably provokes a severe whipping. A child, moreover, must keep absolute silence in the presence of his father or grandfather unless he is called upon to make some remark. Whenever a child sees a person who lacks an ear or a lip, his father reinforces the taboo against verbal insults by telling him that the mutilation is a consequence of something which the unfortunate person said. Especially taboo are such specific epithets as: "The origin of your mother's or father's genitals," "May your ancestral spirits chew their own heads," and "May your ancestral spirits take their bones and eat them." A woman who calls a man a fool is severely punished and may even be killed. To say anything at all that might give offense to another, whether with or without good cause, is to incur liability for conciliation money. Gossiping, tale-bearing, lying, and ridicule are serious breaches of etiquette. The offender's face is smeared with charcoal and he is compelled to parade through the town, holding a live fowl between his teeth and beating a gong, so that everyone may be on hand and make sport. If the offense is committed against a high official, the deed smacks of treason and the culprit, depending upon the seriousness of the insult, either has his lips cut off or is executed. Incidentally, the shame which is apparently felt by the native when he does openly transgress these mores appears to be crystallized in the procedure stereotyped for the licensed tale-bearer whose business it is to gather all the scandal and retail it to the chief. The tale-bearer is evidently not supposed to be very happy about his trade and makes all kinds of excuses for his conduct:

How strongly the innate repugnance of such conduct was ingrained in their code of social conduct may be seen from the ceremony which the licensed tale-bearer had to perform, even under these privileged circumstances. Before making his report, the tale-bearer had to say . . . (I draw a line down my nose that I may speak) or (Ashes lie upon this, my nose, like the white nosed . . . monkey). (131, pp. 328–329)

Certain other acts are also looked upon as insulting. To stare in a person's face, unless actually addressing him, is extremely disrespectful. To break wind in public is an insult not to be tolerated. The following case is recorded by the ethnographer:

During the visit of a person of considerable importance, who was much beloved by the loyal and generous-hearted Ashanti, the Chief and Elders of a remote province, in common with many others, had come to do him honour. When it came to the turn of a certain old man to be presented, in bending forward to do obeisance, he, unnoticed by all but his immediate followers, inadvertently broke wind. Within an hour of the termination of the ceremony he had gone and hanged himself. He had "disgraced" himself and his following. The universal comment in Ashanti among his fellow countrymen was that he had done the only right thing under the circumstances. He could never have lived down the ridicule which he might otherwise have incurred. (131, pp. 372–373)

For a woman to give birth to a monstrosity or a deformed child is to insult her husband and his family. For this reason, about the eighth month of pregnancy, she returns to the village of her own family to await confinement in her mother's house.

The reason stated for this custom was the always present dread that she might be going to bring forth some monstrosity. Among her own clanfolk this would be kept a secret, and so ridicule or other consequences to her husband's people would be avoided. There are traditions of women having given birth to children half human half monkey, half man half fish, children with three or more breasts, six or more toes. All such would, of course, be destroyed, as also hermaphrodites. (132, p. 56)

Stealing is a violation of property rights and as such is severely punished by the Ashanti. A special weapon made of antelope skin is used to whip a child if he takes the most trifling article from his parents. Should he take something of consequence from any member of the family circle, red peppers are inserted in his anus to remind him not to steal in the future. Later in life, theft within the immediate kin-group is not brought to the notice of the chief or council. For the first offense the stolen article is suspended from the thief's neck and he is forced to parade through the town. For a second offense the thief is required to walk naked around the town exposed to the ridicule of his fellows. For the third offense there is a sort of generalized punishment which consists in permitting others to call him a thief and to flog him if he is found on their farm.

When something is stolen by a member of one group from a member of another, the matter is more serious and tends to involve the rival groups.

Even in such cases, however, the Chief was not necessarily called upon to adjudicate between the parties. The heads of the families concerned were at perfect liberty to settle the matter between themselves. In these disputes the house-father and kindred might repudiate the act of their kinsman and hand him over to the injured group, whose slave . . . he would then become. One of my informants stated, "It is much more serious to steal something from someone not belonging to one's own *abusua* than to take from one's own kinsman. The former conduct will give the whole of your kindred a bad name, and the offender will be much more severely dealt with." (131, p. 324)

Theft from a high official, from the dead, or from the gods is regarded as the violation of a national taboo. A court trial followed by execution is the penalty for such an act.

The Ashanti regard adultery as the theft of a prerogative gained by marriage. Punishment varies with the status of the outraged party. Adultery with the wife of an ordinary subject is either ignored or is paid for in conciliation money. If a high official is victimized, the picture is entirely changed. This behavior cannot be due to possible complications in succession arising from an adulterous intrigue, since the son of a king or chief does not succeed to his father's office. The Ashanti seem rather to regard such adultery not only as theft but also as an aggressive act directed against the authorities.

We now come to the last class of "sexual offences" with which the central authority concerned itself, for which the punishment was death. We are here immediately reminded curiously of one of the clauses in our own law of treason, which decrees the death penalty for any one violating the consort of the reigning sovereign (while a similar act against the wife of peer or commoner is not regarded in our law as a capital offence), for in both these respects the Ashanti law seemed almost identical with ours in conception and practice. (131, p. 306)

If the injured official happens to be the war-chief, a knife is thrust through the adulterer's cheeks, his body is pierced with porcupine quills, his genitals are amputated and nailed to a tree, and he is then decapitated. The co-partner of the crime is also put to death. Adultery with the wife of a king is followed by even more elaborate and gruesome punishment prior to execution. To dream of an adulterous union with the wife of a high official brings down punishment upon the offender should even the whisper of his dream experience leak out.

Even in the case of adultery with the wife of a commoner an admixture of aggression aggravates the crime. The forcible seduction of a married woman is punished with death. Adultery with a pregnant woman, moreover, is held to be murder because it is believed to result in the death of the unborn child. Interesting in this connection is the fact that for a widow to have sexual intercourse within a year after the death of her spouse is looked upon as an aggressive act against her dead husband; it so infuriates the deceased that he comes and sleeps with her, causing her either to become barren or to die.

Incest, which would seem at first glance to be a purely sexual offense, is regarded by the Ashanti to some extent as an act of aggression. It is regarded with especial horror and is believed to result in the most disastrous consequences: rain will cease to fall, crops will fail, game will become scarce, and people will be stricken with disease. Incest is an attack upon the ancestors and the gods, and in revenge they inflict all manner of evil upon the entire community; it is regarded, therefore, as an attempt to destroy the group and is punished with death.

This brief review of offenses in Ashanti reveals that most forbidden acts seem to contain a high component of aggression. There can be little doubt that the natives are strongly instigated to aggression. Equally apparent is the social necessity of inhibiting this aggression. Powerful in-group antagonisms, unless held in check by societal control, would probably be sufficient to disorganize completely the political and economic structure of the group.

OUTLETS FOR AGGRESSION

ACCORDING to the hypothesis, there is a strong tendency for inhibited direct aggression to be displaced, i.e., not to disappear but to be expressed in altered form or to be directed toward individuals who were not the source of the frustration. It should be difficult, therefore, for a society to stifle all expressions of aggression. The expression of any form of aggression which is not dangerous to the society should have a cathartic effect and tend to reduce the strength of the instigation to other, more socially dangerous forms of aggression. It will be advantageous to any society, therefore, to permit the expression of certain forms of aggression.

Ashanti culture provides permissive outlets for aggression. There are special occasions when individuals may be angry and express insults. Public punishment of offenders would appear to serve as an outlet for inhibited aggression. A considerable amount of vicarious enjoyment seems to be obtained from watching public executions and from viewing the funeral sacrifices which occur upon the death of a chief. Rattray specifically reports that many of the natives seem to regard these executions and sacrifices with blood-thirsty enjoyment and to derive immense pleasure from observing acts of cruelty righteously inflicted. Sometimes the onlookers join in and play a more direct part in the killing:

> There were undoubtedly a certain number of persons killed, during the first few days after the death was made public, by persons who had worked themselves up into a state of frenzy, and by some psychological process, which I do not pretend to understand, seemed to find in promiscuous killing the only satisfactory relief to their emotions. (132, p. 109)

A possible function of such occasions as these is the catharsis of pent-up aggression which might otherwise break through the bonds of social control.

A further indirect means of expressing aggression is provided in the person of the court jester. This person, usually a dwarf or hunchback, is permitted to make fun even of the king himself, to the obvious enjoyment of the natives. It is obligatory, furthermore, to tell a blood-relative if anyone has slandered him or done anything to his detriment. A nephew, in particular, must tell his maternal uncle if anything of the sort happens. This seems calculated to give individuals some outlet for their aggression as well as to afford a means of consolidating the bonds of the blood group.

A father is obliged to whip his child if the latter is naughty. His neighbors force him to do so if in their opinion the child deserves to be punished; they ridicule him as a man who does not know how to bring up his children. Punishment of children thus appears to be an outlet for the aggression of the parent. The father who wishes to be well thought of by his neighbors and finds his son acting in such a way as to bring ridicule upon him becomes angry with his child. Instead of being blocked from expressing his aggression, he is actually urged by his neighbors to chastise the naughty child. It would seem in this case that aggressive acts were being employed by society to control forbidden acts.

Story-telling also provides a means of aggression. The recounter prefaces his tale with a public statement that what he is about to say is not true, thus apparently absolving both himself and his listeners from any responsibility for the insults which are about to be enjoyed. Subjects ordinarily regarded as sacred, e.g., the gods, the spirit ancestors, the sick, and high officials, appear to be treated as if profane and sometimes even become the subject of ridicule. A period of license seems to prevail on story-telling occasions. Often, in the very middle of a story, actors enter the circle and give impersonations of various characters in the stories, evoking roars of laughter from all witnesses. Rattray recounts an interesting experience in this connection:

On one occasion—it was in connexion, I think with a sketch depicting an old man covered with yaws—I asked someone seated beside me if people habitually laughed at persons inflicted by Nyame (the Sky-god) in this way, and I suggested it was unkind to ridicule such a subject. The person addressed replied that in every day life no one might do so, however great the inclination to laugh might be. . . . Those occasions gave everyone an opportunity of talking about and laughing at such things; it was good for everyone concerned, he said. (133, p. xi)

In addition to the story-telling occasions there is a peculiar ceremony, held once a year, whose function seems almost entirely that of permitting the expression of aggression. During this ceremony everyone is permitted to tell anyone else, including the king himself, what he thinks of him. Some sexual license is permitted, and no redress for seduction or adultery may be claimed throughout the eight days of the ceremony. According to the principle of catharsis, such expressions of aggression should reduce the strength of instigation to aggression; and the reason given by an old priest for this ceremony suggests that this is the probable effect:

You know that everyone has a sunsum (soul) that may get hurt or knocked about or become sick, and so make the body ill. Very often, although there may be other causes, e.g., witchcraft, ill health, this is caused by the evil and hate that another has in his head against you. Again, you too may have hatred in your head against another, because of something that person has done to you, and that, too, causes your sunsum to fret and become sick. Our forebears knew this to be the case, and so they ordained a time, once every year, when every man and woman, free man and slave, should have freedom to speak out just what was in their head, to tell their neighbors just what they thought of them, and of their actions, and not only their neighbors, but also the king or chief. When a man has spoken freely thus, he will feel his sunsum cool and quieted, and the sunsum of the other person against whom he has now openly spoken will be quieted also. (130, pp. 153–154)

In time of war, despite the delay in killing the foe, fierceness of combat is strictly enjoined.

The punishment for cowardice in the presence of the enemy was generally death, but if commuted for a money payment, the man was dressed in woman's waist-beads . . ., his hair dressed in the manner called *atiremmusem* . . ., his eyebrows were shaved off . . ., and any man was at liberty to seduce the coward's wife without the husband being able to claim adultery damages. (131, p. 126)

Warriors are permitted to curse indiscriminately during the campaign. They may insult the chief, the ancestors, and the gods without expecting retaliation. The customs preceding departure for war may perhaps be regarded as unusual frustrations that function to increase the aggression of the warriors. After war is declared, chiefs and soldiers are not permitted to cut their hair or to shave. On the eve of departure to a campaign the warriors take an oath which is generally somewhat as follows:

"I speak the forbidden name of —— I speak the great forbidden name that, if I do not go to this war on which you have sent me forth, or if I go and show my back to the enemy, if I send a bullet and it falls short, and I do not follow it, and if I run away, then have I violated the great forbidden name of ——." (131, p. 123)

After taking such an oath, it is taboo to sleep again in the town and sexual intercourse is forbidden. The chief and his men move to a war-camp and remain there until they set out to war. Routine goal-responses thus suffer interference and increased aggression would be expected to result.

If the frustration-aggression hypothesis is valid, there should be specific adaptations in the way of additional controls of or outlets for aggression during crises of frustration. A seemingly good example is afforded by the customs surrounding the death of an infant. Since the Ashanti are extremely fond of children and since it is well-nigh imperative for prestige purposes that parents have children, the loss of a child soon after birth would seem to be a definite frustration. Eight days must elapse after the birth of a child before the parents make any official claim to the infant. During this period the infant is wrapped in ordinary fiber, customarily only used for sanitation purposes, is given an old mat to lie on, and is not permitted out of doors. On the eighth day comes a celebration during which the child is formally claimed by the parents; it is given its name, dressed in fine cloths, placed upon an expensive mat, and taken out of doors. From the moment of birth, plans are made for the celebration of this rite. Death of the infant before this ceremony occurs would seem to constitute an especially cruel and heartbreaking frustration. Therefore, in accordance with the hypothesis, the parents should be exceptionally aggressive at this time. As a matter of fact, the customary procedure at the death of an infant seems well adapted to a violent expression of aggression.

If an infant dies before the ceremony, the parents become genuinely angry. They whip the little body, mutilate it, wrap it in sharp-cutting spear grass, and place it in a pot which they bury in the women's latrine. The parents shave their heads, dress in white, and partake of groundnut soup, all of which are unpardonable insults at any funeral. A further target for their aggression is the ghost-mother who is believed to have sent the child to the parents in the first place and who has now been so mean as to take it back. The parents retire to their sleeping-compartment and make pretence of lying together. This act is never permitted until forty days after the birth of the child, but is performed in this case to disgrace the ghost-mother who has thus betrayed them.

Another interesting instance of an apparent cultural provision of catharsis for aggression during crises of frustration is given during childhood. When a boy is three years old he sleeps with his father, upon whom now devolves the duty of training the child not to wet the bed at night. This may be regarded as a frustrating experience for the child. It means that when he wishes to relieve his bladder he must control himself long enough to call out to his father and be taken outside the hut. This is a delay interposed between instigation and goal-response. Aggression is aroused in the child against his father, who is the immediate agency of control.

This tendency, however, cannot be expressed, since a child is forbidden to react with hostility toward his parent. Should he be aggressive toward his father, the latter will punish him. Interestingly enough, persistent bed-wetters form the target for the aggression which is apparently engendered in those who receive this and perhaps other frustrations. The children who acquire the habit of not wetting the bed form a group whose privilege it is to ridicule a child who does not accept the cleanliness training. The bed-wetter is caught by the others, tied by them in his bed-mat, taken to the bush, and dressed in a kind of nettle. The boys and girls throw water over him and sing:

> You wash your sleeping mat in the night
> You wash your mat in the night.

If this ridicule succeeds in teaching him not to soil his mat, he then becomes a member of the privileged group and will in turn vent insults upon some other offender. What appears to take place may be interpreted as follows. Aggression is instigated in the child against those of his own age who ridicule and thereby frustrate him. Anticipation of further punishment at their hands inhibits him from expressing aggression toward the group. His aggression is therefore displaced to another delinquent with the approval of both the parent and the group to which he now belongs; i.e., the displacement is rewarded and therefore is reinforced. The child is lined up on the side of the mores. The instigation to aggression generated by the frustrations of social control produces aggression in a form and direction approved by the society, namely, the discipline of another bed-wetter.

In this summary of the Ashanti, an attempt has been made to use the frustration-aggression hypothesis as a basis for organizing certain aspects of the anthropological materials. It has been pointed out that Ashanti society tends to taboo at least the most destructive manifestations of in-group antagonism and at the same time provides certain outlets for inhibited aggression. The tendency of individuals to express aggression presents to Ashanti society a problem which it must solve. Those forms of aggression dangerous to group welfare are strictly prohibited and heavily sanctioned. Aggressive manifestations, on the other hand, are permitted within the group wherever they are consistent with group welfare and they are enjoined in war where the expression of aggression serves a socially useful end.

REFERENCES

References marked with an asterisk (*) are in preparation for publication in psychological journals.

1. ABRAHAM, K. *Versuch einer Entwicklungsgeschichte der Libido.* Vienna: Internationaler Psychoanalytischer Verlag, 1924.

2. ACHILLES, P. S. *The Effectiveness of Certain Social Hygiene Literature.* New York: American Social Hygiene Association, 1923.

3. ACKERSON, L. *Children's Behavior Problems. I. Incidence, Genetic and Intellectual Factors.* Chicago: University of Chicago Press, 1931.

4. AICHHORN, A. *Wayward Youth.* New York: Viking, 1935.

5. ALEXANDER, F. and STAUB, H. *The Criminal, the Judge, and the Public.* New York: Macmillan, 1931.

6. ALLEN, E. (ed.) *Sex and Internal Secretions.* Baltimore: Williams and Wilkins, 1932.

7. ALLPORT, G. W. *Personality: A Psychological Interpretation.* New York: Henry Holt, 1937.

8. AVERILL, L. A. *Adolescence.* Boston: Houghton Mifflin, 1936.

9. BALDWIN, B. T. Physical Growth of Children from Birth to Maturity. *University of Iowa Studies in Child Welfare,* 1921, *1*, No. 1.

10. BARNHART, J. D. Rainfall and the Populist Party in Nebraska. *Amer. pol. Sci. Rev.,* 1925, *19*, 527–540.

11. BELL, H. M. *Youth Tell Their Story.* Washington: American Council on Education, 1938.

12. BELLIS, C. J. Reaction Time and Chronological Age. *Proc. Soc. exp. Biol. Med., N.Y.,* 1932–33, *30*, 801–803.

13. BELSTLER, H. Vierjahresplan und Schule. *Die Scholle,* 1937, *13*, 553–614.

14. BENDER, L., KEISER, S. and SCHILDER, P. Studies in Aggressiveness. *Genet. Psychol. Monog.,* 1936, *18*, 357–564.

15. BEYNON, E. D. Crime and Custom of the Hungarians of Detroit. *J. crim. Law Criminol.,* 1934–35, *25*, 755–774.

16. BODER, D. P. and BEACH, E. V. Wants of Adolescents: I. A Preliminary Study. *J. Psychol.,* 1937, *3*, 505–511.

17. BOLDYREFF, J. W. Recent Materials on Competition and Cooperation in Russia (esp. abstracted articles on N. Plevko, A. P.

Palei, S. Tscherbakoff and N. Konopleff, I. Fleroff, S. Dinamoff, S. S. Molojavy, Zeitlina, S. Mukhin, N. Selezneff, and P. Glago-leff). In *Memorandum on Research in Competition and Coopera-tion*. New York: Social Science Research Council, 1937. Pp. 3–5, 12–14.

18. BONGER, W. A. *Criminality and Economic Conditions*. Boston: Little, Brown, 1916.

19. BONGER, W. A. *An Introduction to Criminology*. London: Me-thuen, 1936.

20. BRADY, R. A. *The Spirit and Structure of German Fascism*. New York: Viking, 1937.

21. BREARLEY, H. C. *Homicide in the United States*. Chapel Hill: University of North Carolina Press, 1932.

22. BRIDGES, K. M. B. Factors Contributing to Juvenile Delin-quency. *J. crim. Law Criminol.*, 1926–27, *17*, 531–580.

23. BRONNER, A. F. Effect of Adolescent Instability on Conduct. *Psychol. Clin.*, 1914–15, *8*, 249–265.

24. BROOKS, F. D. *The Psychology of Adolescence*. Boston: Hough-ton Mifflin, 1929.

25. BRUCE, A. A. One Hundred Years of Criminological Develop-ment in Illinois. *J. crim. Law Criminol.*, 1933–34, *24*, 11–49.

26. BÜHLER, C. The Social Behavior of Children. In, Murchison, C. (ed.) *Handbook of Child Psychology*. (Revised Edition). Worces-ter, Mass.: Clark University Press, 1933.

27. BÜHLER, C. *From Birth to Maturity*. London: Kegan Paul, Trench, Trubner, 1935.

28. BUGELSKI, R. and MILLER, N. E. A Spatial Gradient in the Strength of Avoidance Responses. *J. exp. Psychol.*, 1938, *23*, 494–505.

29. CANNON, W. B. *Bodily Changes in Pain, Hunger, Fear and Rage*. (Second Edition). New York: Appleton, 1929.

30. CASON, H. Common Annoyances: A Psychological Study of Every-day Aversions and Irritations. *Psychol. Monog.*, 1930, *40*, No. 2.

31. Childrens Bureau. Infant Care. *Childrens Bureau Publication No. 8*. Washington: United States Department of Labor, 1938.

32. CRAMPTON, C. W. Physiological Age. *Amer. phys. Educ. Rev.*, 1908, *13*, 144–154; 214–227; 268–283; 345–358.

33. DAVENPORT, F. I. Adolescent Interests. A Study of the Sexual

Interests and Knowledge of Young Women. *Arch. Psychol., N.Y.,* 1923, *10,* No. 66.

34. DOLL, E. A. The Relation of Intelligence to Criminality. *J. soc. Psychol.,* 1930, *1,* 527–531.

35. DOLLARD, J. *Caste and Class in a Southern Town.* New Haven: Yale University Press, 1937.

36. DOOB, L. W. *Propaganda.* New York: Henry Holt, 1935.

37. DOOB, L. W. and SEARS, R. R. Factors Determining Substitute Behavior and the Overt Expression of Aggression. *J. abn. (soc.) Psychol.,* 1939, *34.*

38. ELLIS, H. *The Criminal.* (Fourth Edition). London: Walter Scott, 1910.

38a. ERICKSON, E. H. Observations on Sioux Education. *J. gen. Psychol.* (In press).

39. ERICKSON, M. H. A Study of the Relationship Between Intelligence and Crime. *J. crim. Law Criminol.,* 1928–29, *19,* 592–635.

40. FENICHEL, O. *Hysterien und Zwangsneurosen.* Vienna: Internationaler Psychoanalytischer Verlag, 1931.

41. FERNALD, M. R., HOLMES, M., HAYES, S., and DAWLEY, A. *A Study of Women Delinquents in New York State.* New York: Century, 1920.

42. FIELD, G. L. *The Syndical and Corporative Institutions of Italian Fascism.* New York: Columbia University Press, 1938.

43. FIRTH, R. W. *We the Tikopia.* London: Allen and Unwin, 1936.

44. Fortune Quarterly Survey: XIII. *Fortune,* 1938, *18,* (July), 36.

45. FOSTER, J. C. and ANDERSON, J. E. The Young Child and His Parents. *University of Minnesota Institute of Child Welfare Monograph Series, No. 1.* Minneapolis: University of Minnesota Press, 1930.

46. FREUD, S. Mourning and Melancholia. (1917). Reprinted in *Collected Papers.* London: Hogarth Press, 1934. Vol. IV.

47. FREUD, S. *A General Introduction to Psychoanalysis.* (Trans. by G. S. Hall). New York: Boni and Liveright, 1920.

48. FREUD, S. *Beyond the Pleasure Principle.* London: International Psychoanalytical Press, 1922.

49. FREUD, S. *Civilization and Its Discontents.* (Trans. by Joan Riviere). London: Hogarth Press, 1930.

50. GILLIN, J. L. Some Economic Factors in the Making of the Criminal. *J. soc. Forces,* 1923–24, *2,* 689–691.

51. GILLIN, J. L. Economic Factors in the Making of Criminals. *J. soc. Forces*, 1924–25, *3*, 248–255.

52. GILLIN, J. L. Backgrounds of Prisoners in the Wisconsin State Prison and of Their Brothers. *Amer. sociol. Rev.*, 1937, *2*, 204–212.

53. GLUECK, S. and GLUECK, E. T. *One Thousand Juvenile Delinquents*. Cambridge, Mass.: Harvard University Press, 1934.

54. GOODENOUGH, F. L. *Anger in Young Children*. Minneapolis: University of Minnesota Press, 1931.

55. GORER, G. *Himalayan Village*. London: Michael Joseph, 1938.

56. GORING, C. *The English Convict*. London: H. M. Stationery Office, 1913.

57. HACKER, E. Criminality and Immigration. *J. crim. Law Criminol.*, 1929–30, *20*, 429–438.

58. HANDY, W. C. Native Culture of the Marquesas. *Bull. Bishop Museum*. Honolulu: Bishop Museum, 1923.

59. HARTSHORNE, E. Y., JR. *The German Universities and National Socialism*. Cambridge, Mass.: Harvard University Press, 1938.

60. HARVEY, O. L. The Questionnaire as Used in Recent Studies of Human Sexual Behavior. *J. abn. soc. Psychol.*, 1931–32, *26*, 379–389.

61. HEALY, W. *The Individual Delinquent*. Boston: Little, Brown, 1929.

62. HEALY, W. and BRONNER, A. F. *New Light on Delinquency and Its Treatment*. New Haven: Yale University Press, 1936.

63. HEIMANN, E. *Communism, Fascism, or Democracy?* New York: Norton, 1938.

64. HOLLINGWORTH, L. S. *The Psychology of the Adolescent*. New York: Appleton, 1928.

65. HOOVER, C. B. *Germany Enters the Third Reich*. New York: Macmillan, 1933.

66. HOOVER, C. B. *Dictators and Democracies*. New York: Macmillan, 1937.

67. HORNEY, K. *The Neurotic Personality of Our Time*. New York: Norton, 1937.

68. HOVLAND, C. I. and SEARS, R. R. Experiments on Motor Conflict. I. Types of Conflict and Their Modes of Resolution. *J. exp. Psychol.*, 1938, *23*, 477–493.

69. HOVLAND, C. I. and SEARS, R. R. Minor Studies of Aggression: VI. Correlation of Lynchings with Economic Indices.*

70. HULL, C. L. Goal Attraction and Directing Ideas Conceived as Habit Phenomena. *Psychol. Rev.*, 1931, *38*, 487–506.

71. JAMES, W. *The Principles of Psychology*. (Two Vols.) New York: Henry Holt, 1890.

72. JERSAWIT, V. A. Adolescent "Discontents"—As They Voice Them. *Child Study*, 1932, *9*, 228.

73. JUNOD, H. A. *The Life of a South African Tribe. I. Social Life.* (Revised Edition). London: Macmillan, 1927.

74. KAHN, E. and COHEN, L. H. Organic Drivenness: A Brain-stem Syndrome and an Experience. *N. E. J. Med.*, 1934, *210*, 748–756.

75. KATZ, S. E. and LANDIS, C. Psychologic and Physiologic Phenomena During a Prolonged Vigil. *Arch. Neurol. Psychiat., Chicago*, 1935, *34*, 307–316.

76. KATZ, D. and SCHANCK, R. L. *Social Psychology*. New York: Wiley, 1938.

77. KELLER, A. G. *Societal Evolution*. (Revised Edition). New York: Macmillan, 1931.

78. KILMER, T. W. A Study of the Human Ear from the Standpoint of Identification and Criminality. *Correction*, 1932, *2*, 12.

79. KNIGHT, R. P. The Psychoanalytic Treatment in a Sanatorium of Chronic Addiction to Alcohol. *J. Amer. med. Ass.*, 1938, *111*, 1443–1448.

80. KÖHLER, B. *Des Führers Wirtschaftspolitik*. Munich: Eher, 1935.

81. KOLB, L. Drug Addiction in Its Relation to Crime. *Ment. Hyg., N.Y.*, 1925, *9*, 74–89.

82. LASKER, B. *Race Attitudes in Children*. New York: Henry Holt, 1929.

83. LASSWELL, H. D. *Propaganda Technique in the World War*. New York: Knopf, 1927.

84. LASSWELL, H. D. *Psychopathology and Politics*. Chicago: University of Chicago Press, 1930.

85. LEAL, M. A. Physiological Maturity in Relation to Certain Characteristics of Boys and Girls: A Study of School Children in New Britain, Conn. Philadelphia: Ph.D. Thesis deposited in University of Pennsylvania Library, 1929.

86. Leighton, J. A. *Social Philosophies in Conflict*. New York: Appleton-Century, 1937.

87. Lenin, V. I. The State and Revolution. Reprinted in *Collected Works*. New York: International Publishers, 1932. Vol. 21.

88. Levy, D. M. Thumb or Finger Sucking from the Psychiatric Angle. *Child Develpm.*, 1937, *8*, 99–101.

89. Levy, D. M. and Tulchin, S. H. The Resistance of Infants and Children during Mental Tests. *J. exp. Psychol.*, 1923, *6*, 304–322.

90. Lewin, K. Environmental Forces. (Trans. by D. K. Adams). In, Murchison, C. (ed.) *A Handbook of Child Psychology*. (Revised Edition). Worcester, Mass.: Clark University Press, 1933.

91. Linton, R. Culture, Society and the Individual. *J. abn. soc. Psychol.*, 1938, *33*, 425–436.

92. Lippman, H. S. The Neurotic Delinquent. *Amer. J. Orthopsychiat.*, 1937, *7*, 114–121.

93. Lipschütz, A. *The Internal Secretions of the Sex Glands*. Baltimore: Williams and Wilkins, 1924.

94. Lynd, R. S. and Lynd, H. M. *Middletown*. New York: Harcourt, Brace, 1929.

95. Lynd, R. S. and Lynd, H. M. *Middletown in Transition*. New York: Harcourt, Brace, 1937.

96. Malinowski, B. *Sex and Repression in Savage Society*. New York: Harcourt, Brace, 1927.

97. Man, E. H. On the Aboriginal Inhabitants of the Andaman Islands. Part I. *J. anthropol. Inst. G. B. I.*, 1882–1883, *12*, 69–116.

98. Marshall, R. Precipitation and Presidents. *The Nation*, 1927, *124*, 315–316.

99. Marx, K. and Engels, F. *Manifesto of Communist Party*. Chicago: Kerr.

100. McDougall, W. *Outline of Psychology*. New York: Scribner's, 1923.

101. Mead, M. *Coming of Age in Samoa*. New York: Morrow, 1928.

102. Mead, M. Social Organization of Manua. *Bull. Bishop Museum*, No. 76. Honolulu: Bishop Museum, 1930.

103. Menninger, K. *Man Against Himself*. New York: Harcourt, Brace, 1938.

104. MILES, W. R. Measures of Certain Human Abilities Throughout the Life Span. *Proc. nat. Acad. Sci., Wash.*, 1931, *17*, 627–633.

105. MILES, W. R. Psychological Factors in Alcoholism. *Ment. Hyg., N.Y.*, 1937, *21*, 529–548.

106. MILLER, N. E. Minor Studies of Aggression: III. Degree of Annoyance as a Function of Strength of Motivation.*

107. MILLER, N. E. A Reply to "Sign-Gestalt or Conditioned Reflex?" *Psychol. Rev.*, 1935, *42*, 280–292.

108. MILLER, N. E. and BUGELSKI, R. Minor Studies of Aggression: IV. Some Effects of Frustrations Experimentally Produced by Unsuccessful Cooperation and Competition.*

109. MILLER, N. E. and BUGELSKI, R. Minor Studies of Aggression: II. The Influence of Frustrations Imposed by the In-Group on Attitudes Expressed Toward Out-Groups.*

110. MILLER, N. E. and DAVIS, M. An Experiment on Fighting Behavior Illustrating Similarity between the Psychoanalytic Concept of Displacement and Transfer of Training.*

111. MILLER, N. E. and GOODYEAR, T. Trial and Error Learning of a Social Response in Rats.*

112. MILLER, N. E., HUBERT, G., and HAMILTON, J. B. Mental and Behavioral Changes Following Male Hormone Treatment of Adult Castration, Hypo-gonadism and Psychic Impotence. *Proc. Soc. exp. Biol. Med.*, 1938, Article 9925.

113. MORGAN, J. J. B. *The Psychology of Abnormal People.* (Second Edition). New York: Longmans, Green, 1936.

114. MORROW, H. Dear Mother: I'm in Jail. *Sat. Eve. Post,* August 22, 1936.

115. MOWRER, O. H. Self-Injury as a "Mechanism of Defence."*

116. MOWRER, O. H. and MOWRER, W. M. Enuresis—A Method for Its Study and Treatment. *Amer. J. Orthopsychiat.*, 1938, *8*, 436–459.

117. MURCHISON, C. *Criminal Intelligence.* Worcester, Mass.: Clark University Press, 1926.

118. MURDOCK, G. P. *Our Primitive Contemporaries.* New York: Macmillan, 1934.

119. MURPHY, G., MURPHY, L. B. and NEWCOMB, T. M. *Experimental Social Psychology.* (Revised Edition). New York: Harper, 1937.

120. NANSEN, F. *Eskimo Life.* (Trans. by Wm. Archer). London: Longmans, Green, 1893.

121. NASH, P. The Place of Religious Revivalism in the Formation of the Intercultural Community on Klamath Reservation. In, Eggan, F. *Social Anthropology of North American Tribes.* Chicago: University of Chicago Press, 1937.

122. NELSON, V. F. *Prison Days and Nights.* Boston: Little, Brown, 1933.

123. NONNENBRUCH, F. *Die Dynamische Wirtschaft.* Munich: Eher, 1936.

124. OGBURN, W. F. *Social Change.* New York: Viking, 1923.

125. PAVLOV, I. P. *Conditioned Reflexes.* (Trans. by G. V. Anrep). Oxford: Oxford University Press, 1927.

126. PIL HER, E. Relation of Mental Disease to Crime. *J. crim. Law Criminol.*, 1930–31, *21*, 212–246.

127. POFFENBERGER, A. T. *Applied Psychology.* New York: Appleton-Century, 1927.

128. POTTER, E. C. The Problem of Women in Penal and Correctional Institutions. *J. crim. Law Criminol.*, 1934–35, *25*, 65–75.

129. RAINEY, H. P. *How Fare American Youth?* New York: Appleton-Century, 1937.

130. RATTRAY, R. S. *Ashanti.* Oxford: The Clarendon Press, 1923.

131. RATTRAY, R. S. *Ashanti Law and Constitution.* Oxford: The Clarendon Press, 1929.

132. RATTRAY, R. S. *Religion and Art in Ashanti.* Oxford: The Clarendon Press, 1927.

133. RATTRAY, R. S. *Akan-Ashanti Folk-Tales.* Oxford: The Clarendon Press, 1930.

134. REUTER, E. B., FOSTER, R. G., MEAD, M. et al. Sociological Research in Adolescence. *Amer. J. Sociol.*, 1936, *42*, 81–94.

135. ROBINSON, J. H. *Readings in European History.* Boston: Ginn, 1904.

136. ROSENZWEIG, S. Types of Reaction to Frustration: A Heuristic Classification. *J. abn. soc. Psychol.*, 1934, *29*, 298–300.

137. ROSS, H. Crime and the Native Born Sons of European Immigrants. *J. crim. Law Criminol.*, 1937–38, *28*, 202–209.

138. SCHALLER, H. *Die Schule im Staate Adolf Hitlers.* Breslau: Korn, 1935.

139. SCHAPERA, I. *Khoisan Peoples of South Africa; Bushmen and Hottentots*. London: Routledge, 1930.

140. SCHIRACH, BALDUR VON. *Die Hitler-Jugend*. Leipzig: Koehler und Amelang, 1934.

141. SCHWAB, S. I. and VEEDER, B. S. *The Adolescent*. New York: Appleton-Century, 1929.

142. SEARS, R. R. Functional Abnormalities of Memory with Special Reference to Amnesia. *Psychol. Bull.*, 1936, *33*, 229–274.

143. SEARS, R. R., HOVLAND, C. I. and MILLER, N. E. Minor Studies of Aggression: I. Measurement of Aggressive Behavior.*

144. SEARS, R. R. and SEARS, P. S. Minor Studies of Aggression: V. Strength of Frustration-Reaction as a Function of Strength of Drive.*

145. SELLIN, T. *Research Memorandum on Crime in the Depression*. New York: Social Science Research Council, 1937.

146. SHALLOO, J. P. Youth and Crime. *Ann. Amer. Acad. polit. soc. Sci.*, 1937, *194*, 79–86.

147. SHAW, C. R. *Delinquency Areas*. Chicago: University of Chicago Press, 1929.

148. SHAW, C. R. and McKAY, H. D. Social Factors in Juvenile Delinquency. Vol. II in, National Commission on Law Observance and Enforcement. *Report on the Causes of Crime*. Washington: U. S. Government Printing Office, 1931.

149. SHIELD, J. A. Twelve Thousand Criminals. *J. crim. Law Criminol.*, 1937–38, *28*, 806–814.

150. SHIRLEY, M. M. *The First Two Years: A Study of Twenty-Five Babies. III. Personality Manifestations*. Minneapolis: University of Minnesota Press, 1933.

151. SHUTTLEWORTH, F. K. Sexual Maturation and the Physical Growth of Girls. *Monog. Soc. Res. Child Develpm.*, 1937, *2*, No. 5.

152. SHUTTLEWORTH, F. K. The Adolescent Period, A Graphic and Pictorial Atlas. *Monog. Soc. Res. Child Develpm.*, 1938, *3*, No. 3.

153. SHUTTLEWORTH, F. K. The Physical and Mental Growth of Girls and Boys Age Six to Nineteen in Relation to Age at Maximum Growth. *Unpublished*.

154. SLAWSON, J. *The Delinquent Boy*. Boston: Badger, 1926.

155. SOLLENBERGER, R. T. The Effect of Male-Hormone on Be-

havior with Special Reference to Adolescence. *Psychol. Bull.*, 1938, *35*, 666.

156. SOLLENBERGER, R. T. The Relationship Between Physiological Maturity and the Interests and Attitudes of Boys.*

157. STEWART, C. A. The Feeding of the Child. *Sigma Xi Quart.*, 1938, *26*, 143–152.

158. STODDARD, G. D. and WELLMAN, B. L. *Child Psychology*. New York: Macmillan, 1934.

159. STONE, C. P. and BARKER, R. G. Aspects of Personality and Intelligence in Post Menarcheal and Premenarcheal Girls of the Same Chronological Ages. *J. comp. Psychol.*, 1937, *23*, 439–455.

160. SULLENGER, T. E. Juvenile Delinquency. A Product of the Home. *J. crim. Law Criminol.*, 1933–34, *24*, 1088–1092.

161. SULLENGER, T. E. Female Criminality in Omaha. *J. crim. Law Criminol.*, 1936–37, *27*, 706–711.

162. SULLENGER, T. E. *Social Determinants in Juvenile Delinquency*. New York: Wiley, 1936.

163. SUMNER, W. G. *Folkways*. Boston: Ginn, 1906.

164. SUMNER, W. G. and KELLER, A. G. *The Science of Society*. (Four Vols.) New Haven: Yale University Press, 1927.

165. SUTHERLAND, E. H. *Principles of Criminology*. Philadelphia: Lippincott, 1934.

166. SUTHERLAND, E. H. Mental Deficiency and Crime. In, Young, K. (ed.) *Social Attitudes*. New York: Henry Holt, 1931.

167. SYMONDS, P. M. Life Problems and Interests of Adolescents. *Sch. Rev.*, 1936, *44*, 506–518.

168. TERMAN, L. M. and MERRILL, M. A. *Measuring Intelligence*. Boston: Houghton Mifflin, 1937.

169. *The World Almanac*. New York: New York World-Telegram, 1937.

170. THOMAS, D. S. *Social Aspects of the Business Cycle*. London: Routledge, 1925.

171. THORNDIKE, E. L. *Animal Intelligence*. New York: Macmillan, 1911.

172. THORNDIKE, E. L. et al. *The Measurement of Intelligence*. New York: Bureau of Publications, Teachers College, Columbia University, 1937.

173. THRASHER, F. *The Gang.* Chicago: University of Chicago Press, 1927.

174. *Time,* 1938, *32,* No. 15 (Oct. 10).

175. TRACY, M. E. *Our Country, Our People, and Theirs.* New York: Macmillan, 1938.

176. U. S. Bureau of the Census. *The Prisoner's Antecedents.* Washington: U. S. Government Printing Office, 1929.

177. VEBLEN, T. *The Theory of the Leisure Class.* New York: Macmillan, 1899.

178. WEBB, S. and WEBB, B. *Soviet Communism: A New Civilisation?* New York: Scribner's, 1936.

179. WEBER, M. *The Protestant Ethic and the Spirit of Capitalism.* London: Allen and Unwin, 1930.

180. *Webster's International Dictionary of the English Language.* Springfield: C. and C. Merriam, 1930.

181. WEIDENSALL, J. *The Mentality of the Criminal Woman.* Baltimore: Warwick and York, 1916.

182. WEISBORD, A. *The Conquest of Power.* New York: Covici-Friede, 1937.

183. WHITE, R. (An abstract of research) Submitted by Ralph White, Iowa Child Welfare Research Station. *Bull. Soc. psychol. Study soc. Issues,* 1938, *2,* (No. 2, Jan.), 19.

184. WICKMAN, E. K. *Children's Behavior and Teachers' Attitudes.* New York: The Commonwealth Fund, 1928.

185. WILLIAMS, F. E. *Adolescence. Studies in Mental Hygiene.* New York: Farrar and Rinehart, 1930.

186. WILLIAMS, F. E. *Russia, Youth and the Present-Day World.* New York: Farrar and Rinehart, 1934.

187. WILLOUGHBY, R. R. Sexuality in the Second Decade. *Monog. Soc. Res. Child Develpm.,* 1937, *2,* No. 3.

188. WOLFF, H. A., SMITH, C. E. and MURRAY, H. A. The Psychology of Humor. *J. abn. soc. Psychol.,* 1934, *28,* 341–365.

189. ZILBOORG, G. Differential Diagnostic Types of Suicide. *Arch. Neurol. Psychiat., Chicago,* 1936, *35,* 270–291.

INDEX

Abraham, K., 64, 191
Accident, 11 n, 111 n
Achilles, P. S., 93, 191
Ackerson, L., 102, 191
Adolescence, 72, 84, 91–109; aggression in, 100–107; changes in capacity, 93–94; cultural nature of, 107–109; frustration in, 94–100; physical changes in, 91–93; physiological changes in, 91–93; socialization in, 72, 94–100, 107–109
Adolescent Study Unit, 93
Adultery, 173, 178, 182–183
Adulthood, 72–76, 84–87, 90, 146–149, 159
Advertising, 113 n, 125
Age and criminality, 117–119
Age grading, 69–71
Aggression, accident, relation to, 11 n, 111 n; in adolescents, 100–107; catharsis of, 27, 50–54, 89–90, 136, 183–190; criminality as, 111–112; definition of, 9–11, 11 n, 111–112, 173; direct, 39–41, 47, 82, 103; displacement of, 22, 27, 40–44, 52–53, 87–90, 105–107, 152; economic cycle and, 30–31, 44, 112–113; experiments on, 27–54; forms of, 10, 26, 27, 32–38, 41–54; genesis of, 11; in Germany, 156, 157–158, 159, 162–165; as goal-response, 9, 11; indirect, 39–41; in-group, 20, 22–23, 86–87, 89–90; inhibition of, 27, 32–38, 39–50, 75–87; instigation to, 9–11, 28–32; instinct theories of, 20, 21–22; in Italy, 156, 158, 159, 162–165; measurement of, 28, 29, 30, 103; as neurotic symptom, 15, 47; non-overt, 32–38, 107; object of, 27, 39–54, 87–90; overt, 32–38, 52, 105, 107; toward parents, 13–15, 48, 78–82, 105; patterning of, 10 n, 22, 87–90; principles of, 27–54; "readiness to," 33, 87–89; regulation of, 75–87; as response to frustration, 1–3, 10–11, 27; in

Russia, 156, 158, 162, 165–166; toward self, 10, 21, 46–50, 128; sociological data and, 143; substitute response and, 9 n; synonyms for, 10; in United States, 156–157, 158–162, 164
Aichhorn, A., 126, 138, 191
Alcoholism, 135
Alexander, F., 121, 138, 191
Algeria, 131
Algesimeter test, 52
Allen, E., 91, 92, 191
Allport, G. W., 37, 191
Anderson, J. E., 76 n, 193
Anger, 77 n
Annoyance, 31, 77 n
Anticipatory goal-response, 34 n
Anxiety, 19
Appearance, personal, 121–123
Ashanti, 172–190
Ashanti, control of aggression among, 173–183, 189–190; outlets for aggression among, 183–190
Assault, physical, 178–179
Austria, 167
Austrians, 162
Autocracy, 88
Avanguardisti, 147
Averill, L. A., 191

Baldwin, B. T., 92, 191
Barker, R. G., 93, 200
Barnhart, J. D., 44, 191
Ba Thonga, 59 n
Beach, E. V., 99, 191
Belgium, 129
Bell, H. M., 95, 97, 98–99, 104, 145, 146, 149, 157, 160, 191
Bellis, C. J., 94, 191
Belstler, H., 157, 160, 191
Bender, L., 130, 191
Beynon, E. D., 125 n, 191
Bill of Rights, 159
Boder, D. P., 99, 191
Boldyreff, J. W., 145, 191–192
Bolsheviks, 148

Bonger, W. A., 112, 113, 114, 126, 129, 131, 135, 136 n, 140, 192
Brady, R. A., 145, 150, 192
Brearley, H. C., 115, 134, 137, 192
Bridges, K. M. B., 122, 125, 126 n, 131, 192
Bronner, A. F., 102, 103, 123–124, 139–141, 192
Brooks, F. D., 94, 100, 192
Bruce, A. A., 137, 192
Bugelski, R., 42–44, 47, 52, 192, 197
Bühler, C., 76, 80, 102, 107, 192

California, 152
Cannon, W. B., 19, 192
Cason, H., 77 n, 192
Catharsis, 27, 50–54, 89–90, 136, 183–190
Chicago, delinquency in, 112
Children, 56–71, 76 n–77 n, 78–87, 88, 144–146, 177–179, 185, 187–189
Childrens Bureau, 59 n, 60, 62, 63, 79, 192
Child training, 57–71; aggression, 78–87; among Ashanti, 177–179, 187–189; cleanliness, 62–64, 76 n, 80, 187–189; feeding, 58–61; masturbation, 66–67, 81–82; sex behavior, 65–68
Class struggle, 23–25
Cohen, L. H., 123, 195
Communism (*see also* Russia), 87
Communist Party, 148, 150, 154
Competition, 159, 165
Conflict, 36–38
Conscience, 86–87, 132
Convicts, 112
Coöperation, antagonistic, 22, 77; and competition, 42–43, 47
Crampton, C. W., 92, 192
Crimes, property, 31
Criminality, 26, 82, 88, 110–141, 162–163; age and, 117–119; alcoholism and, 135; definition of, 137; theory of, 110–112, 138–141; factors in: drug addiction, 135; economic status, 112–113; educational status, 114–116; form of government, 137; health, 123; home conditions, 131–132; hyperactivity, 123–124; illegitimacy, 126–127; intelligence,

116–117; marital status, 127–129; militarism, 135–137; moral holidays, 135–137; nationality, 124–126; neighborhood conditions, 132–133; personal appearance, 121–123; physical defects, 121–123; physical size, 119–121; psychopathology, 137–138; race, 124–126; regional conditions, 133–135; sex ratio, 129–131; vocational status, 113–114
Crow Indians, 61
Crying, 28–29, 62, 65, 79, 83
Cycle, economic, 30–31, 44, 112–113
Czechoslovakia, 167

Davenport, F. I., 95–96, 192–193
Davis, M., 42, 197
Dawley, A., 113, 117, 129 n, 193
Death, 75, 77 n, 128, 188
Death instinct, 22
Defects, physical, 121–123
Delinquency, adolescent, 102–103, 105–106
Delinquency areas, 132–133
Democracy (*see also* United States), 88
Denmark, 131
Dependence, child's, on parents, 64–65
Detective stories, 26, 46, 107
Dewey, J., 145
Diffusion, 173
Disease, 74
Displacement, 2, 22, 27, 40–44, 52–53, 105–107, 152
Divorce, 127
Doll, E. A., 116 n, 193
Dollard, J., 22, 26, 125, 131, 152, 193
Dominance, exploratory, 61–62, 77 n
Doob, L. W., 29, 35, 36, 40, 106, 193
Drug addiction, 135

Education, 144–146, 159
Effect, Law of, 18–19, 33
Ellis, H., 116 n, 121–122, 193
Engels, F., 23–26, 196
Erickson, E. H., 71, 193
Erickson, M. H., 116 n, 127 n, 136 n, 193
Ethiopia, 170

Extinction, experimental, 19, 34 n, 59–60, 65

Failure, 34
Family, 56–71, 78–87, 94–100, 112, 131–132, 147, 151
Fascism (*see also* Germany *and* Italy), 87
Feeblemindedness, 116–117
Feeding, 58–61
Fenichel, O., 68, 80, 193
Fernald, M. R., 113, 117, 129 n, 193
Field, G. L., 150, 193
Finland, 129
Firth, R. W., 48 n, 193
Fortune Quarterly Survey, 164, 193
Foster, J. C., 76 n, 193
Foster, R. G., 95, 198
France, 126
Free association, 32
French, 153
French Canadians, 153
Freud, S. A., 21–22, 40–41, 46–47, 60 n, 63, 67, 81, 90, 135, 193
Frustration, of adolescents, 94–100; agent of, 39–44, 48, 125; aggression as response to, 1–3; in childhood, 56–87; of criminals, 110–141; definition of, 6–7, 10–11; genesis of, 11; in Germany, 149–150, 151; group, 13, 42–43, 87–90, 125; inhibition of aggression as, 40–41, 61, 62, 63, 65, 80–87; in Italy, 149–150, 151; non-aggressive responses to, 19, 138; patterning of, 55–76; Rosenzweig's reaction-types, 50 n; in Russia, 149–150, 151; sociological data and, 143; strength of, 30–31; in United States, 149, 150–151

Generalization, 39 n
Germany, 74, 142–143; aggression in, 156, 157–158, 159, 162–165; economic frustrations of, 149–150; gratifications in, 166–171; race prejudice in, 152, 153–156, 157–158; resocialization in, 147–148; social frustrations of, 151; socialization in, 145, 146
Ghost, 175
Gillin, J. L., 112 n, 113, 129, 193–194

Glueck, S. and E. T., 115 n, 126, 132, 140, 194
Goal-response, aggression as, 11; definition of, 6; experiencing as, 16; interference with, 7–8; and substitute response, 8–9
Gonad, 91–93
Goodenough, F. L., 76 n, 80, 194
Goodyear, T., 37, 197
Gorer, G., 61, 194
Goring, C., 119, 123, 194
Gossip, 179–180
Gratification, in Germany, 166–171; in Italy, 166–171; in Russia, 166–171; in United States, 166–171

Hacker, E., 117, 133, 194
Hamilton, J. B., 93, 197
Handy, W. C., 108, 194
Hartshorne, E. Y., Jr., 145, 194
Harvey, O. L., 92–93, 96, 194
Hayes, S., 113, 117, 129 n, 193
Health, 123
Healy, W., 103, 120, 123–124, 139–141, 194
Heimann, E., 142, 194
Hitler, A., 145, 147, 154, 163–164
Hitler Jugend, 147
Holidays, moral, 135–137
Hollingworth, L. S., 100, 194
Holmes, M., 113, 117, 129 n, 193
Homicide, 15, 134
Homosexuality, 72, 129
Hoover, C. B., 142, 194
Horney, K., 47 n, 75, 194
Housing, 134
Hovland, C. I., 31, 32, 36, 45, 52, 194–195
Hubert, G., 93, 197
Hull, C. L., 34 n, 195
Humor, 26, 32, 45–46, 163, 184–185
Hungary, 74
Hunger, 28–29, 58–61
Hyperactivity, 123–124

Identification, 34
Illegitimacy, 126–127
Illinois Institute for Juvenile Research, 102
Incest, 183
India, 153

Indians, 125

Indians, Crow, 61; Klamath, 173

Individualism, 156–157

In-group, 20, 22–23, 86–87, 89–90, 104, 154

Inhibition, of aggression, 27, 32–38, 39–50, 75–87

Inhibition, sexual, 66–67

Injury, 9–11, 34, 47–49, 52

Insecurity, social, 73–74

Instigation, definition of, 4; to excretion, 62–64; frustration-induced, 9 n; measurement of, 5, 29, 30; reduction of, 8–9, 50–54; secondary, 9 n, 11, 31; strength of, 4–5, 27, 28–32, 39–41; substitute response and, 8–9, 9 n; summation of, 31–32

Instigator, definition of, 3–4

Instincts, 20–21, 22

Insults, 179–181

Intelligence, 116–117

Interference (*see* Frustration)

Inventions, 146–147

Irish, 125, 151

Italians, 125

Italy, 89, 126, 142–143; aggression in, 156, 158, 159, 162–165; economic frustration of, 149–150; gratification in, 166–171; race prejudice in, 151–152, 158; resocialization in, 147–148; social frustrations of, 151; socialization in, 145, 146

James, W., 20, 195

Japanese, 151, 152

Jealousy, sibling, 26, 83

Jersawit, V. A., 99, 195

Jewish Charities, 112

Jews, 32, 87, 148, 154–156, 157–158

Junod, H. A., 59 n, 195

Kahn, E., 123, 195

Katz, D., 139 n, 195

Katz, S. E., 32, 195

Keiser, S., 130, 191

Keller, A. G., 22–23, 57, 128 n, 195

Kilmer, T. W., 122, 195

Klamath Indians, 173

Knight, R. P., 135, 195

Köhler, B., 150, 195

Kolb, L., 135, 195

Labor Front, 150

Landis, C., 32, 195

Lasker, B., 152, 195

Lasswell, H. D., 39–40, 42, 195

Leal, M. A., 106, 195

Learning, 18–19, 39 n, 50 n, 60

Leighton, J. A., 142, 196

Lenin, V. I., 25, 147, 148, 165, 196

Lepchas, 61

Levy, D. M., 59, 80, 196

Lewin, K., 78, 87–88, 196

Linton, R., 69, 196

Lippman, H. S., 138, 196

Lipschutz, A., 92, 196

Lombroso, 122

Love, withdrawal of, 78–80

Lynching, 1, 26, 31, 44, 88

Lynd, R. S. and H. M., 95, 96, 97, 99, 105, 107, 156, 157, 160, 196

Malinowski, B., 108, 196

Man, E. H., 59, 196

Manuans, 59 n

Marquesas, 108

Marriage, 72–73, 95, 127–129

Marshall, R., 44, 196

Marx, K., 22, 23–26, 165, 196

Marxians, 143, 146, 157

Maryland, 97, 98–99

Masochism, 10

Masturbation, 65–68, 72, 81–82

McDougall, W., 20–21, 196

McKay, H. D., 112, 132–133, 199

Mead, M., 59 n, 67, 95, 107, 196

Menninger, K., 47 n, 196

Menshevik, 158

Middletown, 96, 97, 105, 107

Miles, W. R., 94, 135, 197

Militarism, 135–137

Miller, N. E., 29–30, 31, 32, 35, 36, 37, 42–44, 45, 47, 52, 93, 192, 197

Mobility, social, 73–74

Morgan, J. J. B., 32, 197

Morrow, H., 94, 197

Motion pictures, 113 n, 121

Mowrer, O. H., 49, 135, 197

Mowrer, W. M., 135, 197

Murchison, C., 116, 197

Murder, 175–176

Murdock, G. P., 61, 95, 197

Murphy, G. and L. B., 76 n, 197

Murray, H. A., 46 n, 201
Mussolini, B., 145, 167, 168, 169

Nama Hottentot, 59 n
Nansen, F., 59, 198
Nash, P., 173, 198
Nationality, 124–126
National socialism (*see* Germany)
National Youth Commission, 97, 104
Negativism, 76 n–77 n
Negro, 152, 153
Negroes, aggression toward, 22, 44, 87, 125, 133 n; criminality among, 131
Neighborhood, 132–133
Nelson, V. F., 121, 122, 198
Newcomb, T. M., 76 n, 197
New Deal, 147
New Economic Policy, 148
Nonnenbruch, F., 150, 198

Ogburn, W. F., 146, 198
Out-group, 89–90

Patterning, traditional, 152
Pavlov, I. P., 19, 198
Perception, 39 n, 48, 156
Physiology of adolescence, 91–93
Pilcher, E., 115 n, 117, 198
Pituitary gland, 91–92
Plato, 145
Poffenberger, A. T., 98, 198
Poland, 155
Police, 85–86
Politicians, aggression toward, 44, 133 n
Post-encephalitic syndrome, 123–124
Potter, E. C., 131, 198
Poverty, 112–113
Pregnancy, 177–178, 180–181
Prohibition Amendment, 85
Propaganda, 39–41, 169, 170
Prostitution, 130–131
Protestantism, 156–157
Psychopathology, 15, 123–124, 137–138
Pubescence (*see* Adolescence)
Punishment, 184, 185; anticipation of, 19, 21, 27, 32–38, 110–112, 132–133, 138–141; definition of, 34, 110–111 n

Race, 124–126
Race prejudice, 26, 43–44, 82, 89–90; in Germany, 152, 153–156, 157–158; in Italy, 151–152, 158; in Russia, 148, 152; in United States, 151, 152; theory of, 151–153
Radicalism, 139 n
Rainey, H. P., 97, 198
Rattray, R. S., 172–190, 198
Reaction-formation, 130 n
Region, 133–135
Reinforcement, 6, 8, 9, 42, 56, 64
Religion, 169
Repression, 35 n
Resocialization, in Germany, 147–148; in Italy, 147–148; in Russia, 147–148; in United States, 146–147, 148
Reuter, E. B., 95, 198
Ridicule, 179
Rivalry, 152
Robinson, J. H., 89, 198
Röhm, Ernst, 163
Roosevelt, F. D., 46, 164
Rosenzweig, S., 50 n, 198
Ross, H., 125 n, 133, 198
Russia, 74, 108, 142–143; aggression in, 156, 158, 162, 165–166; economic frustrations of, 149–150; gratifications in, 166–171; race prejudice in, 148, 152; resocialization in, 147–148; social frustrations of, 151; socialization in, 145–146

Schaller, H., 145, 198
Schanck, R. L., 139 n, 195
Schapera, I., 59 n, 199
Schilder, P., 130, 191
Schirach, Baldur von, 145, 199
School, 71, 83–84, 113 n, 114–116, 125, 144–146
Schwab, S. I., 91, 199
Sears, P. S., 28–29, 199
Sears, R. R., 28, 29, 31, 32, 34 n, 35, 36, 40, 45, 52, 194, 195, 199
Sellin, T., 113, 199
Senescence, 75, 77 n
Sex, 166–167; and criminality, 126–132
Sex behavior, adolescent, 72, 92–93;

child-parent relations, 67–68, 95–96; inhibition of, 66–67, 94–100; instigation to, 92–93, 98–100

Sex hormone, 93, 101, 103

Sex ratio, 129–131

Sex typing, 68–69

Shalloo, J. P., 199

Shaw, C. R., 112, 132–133, 139, 199

Shield, J. A., 113 n, 115 n, 117 n, 199

Shirley, M. M., 76 n, 199

Shuttleworth, F. K., 92, 99, 199

Size, physical, 119–121

Slawson, J., 120, 199

Sleep-deprivation, 32, 45, 52

Smith, C. E., 46 n, 201

Socialization, of adolescents, 72, 94–100, 107–109; of adults, 72–76; of children, 56–71; definition of, 55–56; as frustration, 56; in Germany, 145, 146; in Italy, 145, 146; regulation of aggression in, 75–87; in Russia, 145–146; in United States, 144–145, 146

Sollenberger, R. T., 93, 103, 105, 199–200

Soviet Union (*see* Russia)

Stakhanovite system, 165

Stalin, J., 147–148

State, 25, 85–86, 137, 148, 164–165, 173

Status, economic, 112–113, 159; educational, 114–116; marital, 127–129; vocational, 113–114

Staub, H., 121, 138

Stealing, 181–182

Stewart, C. A., 61, 200

Stoddard, G. D., 76, 200

Stone, C. P., 93, 200

Story-telling, 185–186

Strike, 150

Substitute response, in adolescence, 107; definition of, 8–9; development of, 58, 81, 101–102

Sudetenland, 170

Sudetens, 162

Suicide, 10, 21, 26, 47–48, 173–174, 177

Sullenger, T. E., 110, 113 n, 123, 126, 131, 200

Sumner, W. G., 22–23, 77, 87, 89, 128 n, 200

Supreme Court, 159

Sutherland, E. H., 114, 115, 116, 117, 119, 122, 123, 124, 125, 129, 131, 135, 138, 200

Symonds, P. M., 100, 200

Syndicates, 150

Taboo, 67, 86, 89, 91, 95, 108, 136, 165, 178, 179, 189–190

Teachers College, 144

Terman, L. M., 94, 200

Terrill, R., 46 n

Thomas, D. S., 31, 47, 200

Thorndike, E. L., 18, 94, 200

Thrasher, F., 104, 201

Thumb-sucking, 59–60

Tikopia, 48

Time, 85, 201

Tracy, M. E., 142, 145, 150, 158, 163, 166, 167, 168, 170, 201

Trait, 37

Treason, 173

Trotskyites, 148

Tulchin, S., 80

Unemployment, 149

United Charities, 112

United States, 142–143; aggression in, 156–157, 158–162, 164; economic frustrations of, 149; gratifications in, 166–171; race prejudice in, 151, 152; resocialization in, 146–147, 148; social frustrations of, 150–151; socialization in, 144–145, 146

U. S. Dept. of Commerce, 115, 127, 136, 201

Urban II, Pope, 89 n

Veblen, T., 74, 201

Veeder, B. S., 91, 199

Versailles, treaty of, 153, 154

Vienna, 170

War, 1, 26, 39–41, 74, 164, 167–168, 173–175, 176–177, 186–187

Weaning, 58–61

Webb, S. and B., 148, 150, 165, 170, 201

Weber, M., 156–157, 201

Webster's International Dictionary, 19, 201

Weidenshall, J., 119–120, 201
Weimar, 154
Weisbord, A., 142, 201
Wellman, B. L., 76, 200
White, R., 201
Wickman, E. K., 84, 96, 201

Williams, F. E., 97, 108, 146, 201
Willoughby, R. R., 92, 201
Wolff, H. A., 46 n, 201
World Almanac, 95, 131, 200

Zilboorg, G., 47 n, 201